ART DIRECTORS'
INDEX
TO ILLUSTRATORS
19

RotoVision

CREDITS - COPYRIGHT

COVER ILLUSTRATION

Hamza Arcan

The Studio

1 Salisbury Road

Hove, East Sussex

BN3 3AB. UK

Tel: +44 (0)1273 205030

Fax: +44 (0)1273 205030

COVER DESIGN

CLIVE SPRING &

ROTOVISION SA

PUBLISHER

ROTOVISION SA

7 Rue du Bugnon

CH 1299 Crans

Switzerland

SALES OFFICE:

Sheridan House

112-116A Western Road

Hove

East Sussex

BN3 1DD

United Kingdom

Tel: +44 (0) 1273 727268

Fax: +44 (0) 1273 727269

Email: Sales@RotoVision.com

Website: www.RotoVision.com

COPYRIGHT

© 1999 ROTOVISION SA

ISBN 2-88046-385-8

Printed in Hong Kong

CONTENTS

GERMANY
5-18

LATIN AMERICA
19-22

ARGENTINA
20

BRAZIL
21

SCANDINAVIA
23-72

SPAIN
73-76

UK
77-98

ASSOCIATION OF ILLUSTRATORS, UK
99-344

PORTFOLIO OF PAGE SALES AGENTS

ARGENTINA
Aquiles Ferrario
Documenta SRL
Calle Maipu 763
2do Piso "D"
1006 Buenos Aires
Argentina
Tel: +54 1 14 393 9125
Fax: +54 1 14 326 9595
Email: pedidos@documenta.com.ar

BRAZIL
Hirokazu Taguchi / Rui Nagasawa
Casa Ono Comércio e Importção Ltda
Rua Fernão Dias 492
Pinheiros
CEP 05427
São Paulo SP Brazil
Tel: +55 11 813 6522
Fax: +55 11 813 6921
Contacto Publicitario: Denise Correa
Tel: +55 21 261 0919

GERMANY
Gudrun Tempelmann-Boehr
Am Rosenbaum 7
D-40699 Erkrath
Germany
Tel: +49 211 25 32 46
Fax: +49 211 25 46 32

GERMANY
Margret Ostrowski-Wenzel
Am Weiher 14
D-20255 Hamburg
Germany
Tel: +49 40 40 56 12
Fax: +49 40 40 56 12

ITALY
Zandra Mantilla
Via Monte Amiata 3
I-20149 Milano
Italy
Tel: +39 2 498 4926
     +39 2 480 12684
Fax: +39 2 498 4926
Email: zandrama@tin.it

MEXICO
Guillermo Pérez / María Elena Trujillo
CoEdi Mex SA de CV
Avda Chapultepec # 417 "A" Dto. 5
Colonia Juárez
06600-México DF
Tel: +52 5 207 9991
Fax: +52 5 207 9991

SCANDINAVIA
Barbro Ehn
BOE Media AB
Sibyllegatan 38
114 43 Stockholm
Sweden
Tel: +46 8 661 0069
Fax: +46 8 661 0073

SOUTH AFRICA
Trudy Dickens
Association of Marketers
P.O. Box 98853
Sloane Park
2152 Johannesburg
South Africa
Tel: +27 11 462 2380
     +27 11 706 1633
Fax: +27 11 706 4151

SPAIN
Sylvie Estrada
Index Book SL
Consell de Cent 160 - Local 3
E-08015 Barcelona
Spain
Tel: +34 93 454 5547
Fax: +34 93 454 8438
Email: ib@indexbook.com

SWITZERLAND
Katja Cavazzi
T-Case AG
Zollikerstrasse 19, Postfach
CH-8032 Zürich
Switzerland
Tel: +41 1 383 4680
Fax: +41 1 383 4680

UK
Nicole Harman
RotoVision SA
112/116a Western Road
Hove, East Sussex
BN3 1DD, UK
Tel: +44 (0)1273 716029
Fax: +44 (0)1273 727269
Email: sales@RotoVision.com
Website: www.RotoVision.com

VENEZUELA
Luis Fernandez Ramirez / Alvaro Alvarez
Contemporanea De Ediciones
Avenida La Salle Cruce Con Lima
Edificio Irbia, Urb. Los Caobos
1050 Caracas
Tel: +58 2 793 7591
Fax: + 58 2 793 6566

REGIONAL OFFICES:

ASIA
Alice Goh
ProVision Pte Ltd
34 Wilkie Road
228054 Singapore
Tel: +65 334 7720
Fax: +65 334 7721
Email: aliceg@pacific.net.sg

LATIN AMERICA
Alejandro Christe
Delegación América Latina
Alsina 120
5147 Argüello
Córdoba
Argentina
Tel: +54 3543 420925
Fax: +54 3543 420925
Email: christe@arnet.com.ar

Tempelmann-Boehr | Gudrun 25

Fuhlrott Design 26

Kessler | Maric 27

Thiele | Michael 28

Regös | Ferenc B. 30

Uertz | Peter 31

Büttner | Rolf 32

Kunstmann | Ralf 33

Plikat | Ari 34

Wohlgemuth | Stephan 35

Moos-Drevenstedt | Erika 36

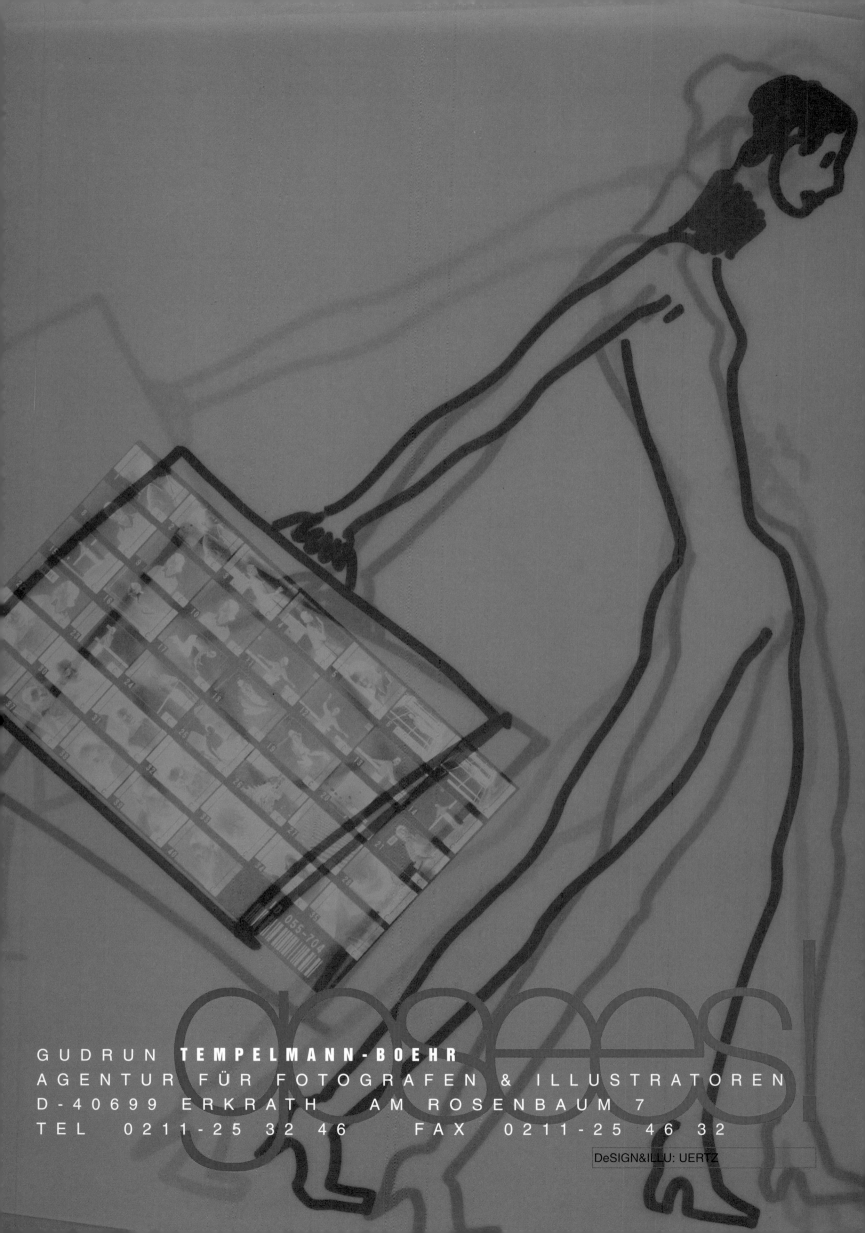

GUDRUN **TEMPELMANN-BOEHR**
AGENTUR FÜR FOTOGRAFEN & ILLUSTRATOREN
D-40699 ERKRATH   AM ROSENBAUM 7
TEL   0211-25 32 46   FAX   0211-25 46 32

DeSIGN&ILLU: UERTZ

DIETMAR FUHLROTT
● ● ● ● ● ● ● ● ● ● ● ●

Fuhlrott Design
Moltkestrasse 24
45128 Essen
Germany
Tel: +49 (0)201 22 14 71
Fax: +49 (0)201 22 14 73

Agent:
Gudrun Tempelmann - Boehr
Agentur für Fotografen und Illustratoren
Am Rosenbaum 7
40699 Erkrath
Germany
Tel: +49 (0)211 25 32 46
Fax: +49 (0)211 25 46 32

Von manuell bis digital
Schwerpunkte: Technik, Architektur, Medizin, Wissenschaft
seit 1975 selbstständig

8

If you run short of time (or ideas) — just call + 49 · (0)8192 · 999101

MARIO KESSLER

Studio Mario Kessler
Am Eichet 12
D-86938 Schondorf
Germany
Tel: +49 (0)8192 99 91 01
Fax: +49 (0)8192 99 91 02

Ideas and Illustrations

MICHAEL THIELE

Dreihüttenstraße 16
D-44135 Dortmund
Tel./Fax: (0231) 52 99 11

Agentur für Fotografen und Illustratoren
GUDRUN TEMPELMANN - BOEHR
Am Rosenbaum 7 - D-44699 Erkrath
Tel. (0211) 25 32 46 - Fax: (0211) 25 46 32

MICHAEL THIELE

Dreihüttenstraße 16
D-44135 Dortmund
Tel./Fax: (0231) 52 99 11

Agentur für Fotografen und Illustratoren
GUDRUN TEMPELMANN - BOEHR
Am Rosenbaum 7 - D-44699 Erkrath
Tel. (0211) 25 32 46 - Fax: (0211) 25 46 32

REGÖS FERENC BÉLA
◆◆◆◆◆◆◆◆◆◆

Ziegeleiweg 6.
82398 Odeerding-Polling G
Germany
Tel: +49 (0)88 1 3677

Diplom-Designer

PETER UERTZ
ILLUSTRATION & MULTIMEDIA
T 49[0]211 5571216   FAX 49[0]211 5571218
E.-MAIL: p_uertz@mail.mcs.de

www.uertz.mcs.de
www.rageagainstmachine.com

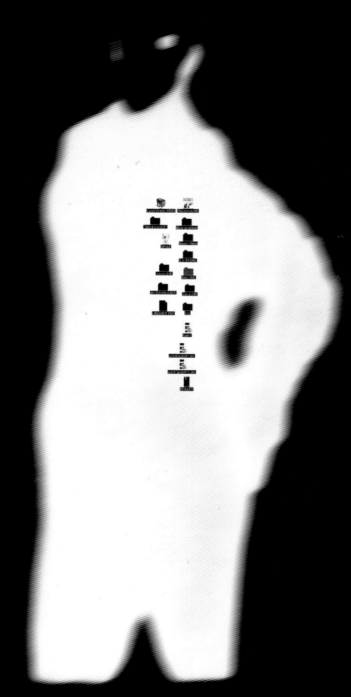

agent: GUDRUN TEMPELMANN-BOEHR
T 49[0]211 25 32 46 FAX 49[0]211 254632
MOBIL: 0172 6290170

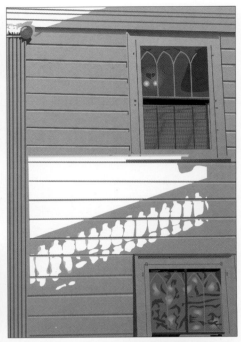

ROLF BÜTTNER
• • • • • • • • • • • • • •

Am Fliegelskamp 27a
D-40885 Ratingen
Germany
Tel: +49 (0)2102 17879
Fax: +49 (0)2102 18411
Email: buettner@mail.mcs.de
www.buettner.de

Free-lance Creative Director
Werbung, grafik, illustrationen, corporate design, cartoons, computer grafik, alle techniken

Agent:
Gudrun Tempelmann - Boehr
Agentur für Fotografen und Illustratoren
Am Rosenbaum 7
40699 Erkrath
Germany
Tel: +49 (0)211 25 32 46
Fax: +49 (0)211 25 46 32

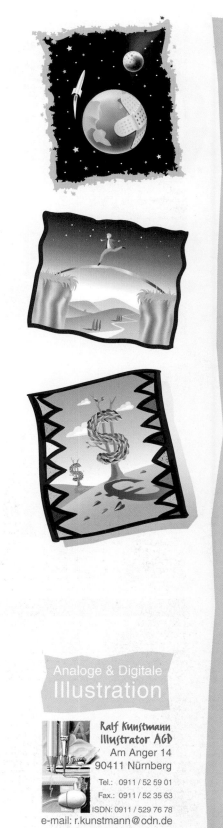

• Vom Webbutton bis zum Fotorealismus •

ARI PLIKAT

Ari Plikat
Haydnstrasse 52
D-44145 Dortmund
Germany
Tel: +49 (0)231 51 52 27
Fax: +49 (0)231 51 59 17

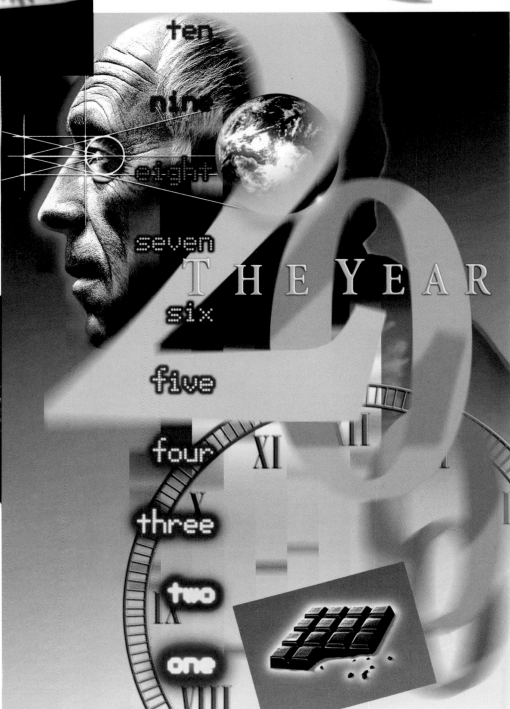

STEPHAN WOHLGEMUTH

wohlgemuth illustriert
Jahrallee 15
65795 Okriftel
Germany
Tel: +49 (0)61 90 71 930
Fax: +49 (0)61 90 73 778

It's a Trick, not a Sony!

36
GE

ERIKA MOOS-DREVENSTEDT
ILLUSTRATION+DESIGN

Paul-Gerhardt-Str.23 / D-47877 Willich
Telefon:+49-(0)2156-3806 / Fax:+49-(0)2156-1380
e-mail: erika@moos-drevenstedt.de
Mobil:+49 (0)172-2105700

Internet: www.moos-drevenstedt.de

Agent:
GUDRUN TEMPELMANN-BOEHR
Am Rosenbaum 7 · D - 40699 Erkrath
Tel.:+49-(0)211-253246 · Fax:+49-(0)211-254632

Freelance since 1969.
Figurative, cartoon, plants, animals, computer.
Many different styles and techniques.

18

ARGENTINA   BRAZIL

I L L U S T R A T I O N

I L U S T R A C I Ó N

●

Estudio T Arte & Animação 21

Lopez Dupuy, Roberto Francisco 20

LOPEZ DUPUY

Dorrego 1209 (2000) Rosario Argentina
TelFax: 54-341-4495970
e-mail:lopezdupuy@arnet.com.ar

Publicidad . Diseño . Campañas Publicitarias y Promociones de Ventas . Identidad Visual Corporativa y Logotipos . Material de Merchandising . Packaging . Folletos . Stands

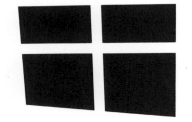
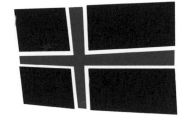
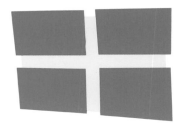

DENMARK   NORWAY   SWEDEN

ILLUSTRATION

●

Almquist, Ulla 25

Andersen, Marita 26, 27

Andersson, Christina 42

Anne Technigar HB 62

Asken Art AB 68, 69

Barsted, Vivi 43

Boge, Bjørn Mike 31

Bok, Bild & Text 35

Carlsson, Catharina 34

CGA Information AB .28, 29

Charlies Bilder AB 64, 65

Deville Design AS 70

East, Stella 44, 45

Flusund, Gunnar 47

Göhlner, Christine 48

Granhaug, Silje 36, 37

Hansson, Stefan 66

Hedegaard Grafisk Design 49

Jägergård, Åsa 50

Johre, Fredrik 51

Jondell, Ingela 40

Juul Jensen, Mikkel 54

Kaj Wistbacka Illustration och Design 71

Karlsen, Hermod 55

Lindahl, Ola 39

Lindroos, Per 52, 53

Lundwall, Bo 57

Meder, Peter 58, 59

Melander, Lars 60, 61

Rykkelid, Gro T. 63

Segelson, Svante 38

Ståhlberg, Harriet 67

Syster Diesel 46

Tegnestven De 5 56

Triffon Arts 32, 33

Waxberg, Cecilia 72

Åbjörnsson Art AB 41

Åvall, Ethel 30

181

SCA

1.

2.

3.

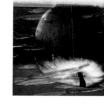

4.

5.

7.

8.

6.

ULLA ALMQUIST

● ● ● ● ● ● ● ● ● ● ● ● ● ● ● ● ● ● ● ●

Almquist AB
Box 35, SE-430 94 Bohus-Björkö, Sweden
Tel: +46 31 92 90 72 Fax/Modem: +46 31 92 90 73
www.almquistab.se E-mail: Ulla.Almquist@almquistab.se

1. Magazine cover
   Client: Mölndals Kommun

2. Course Catalogue
   Client: SIK

3. Newsletter, Folder, Exhibition in Shanghai, Campaign Badge
   Client: The National museums of world culture

4. Postcard
   Client: RBU

5. Postcard
   Client: RBU

6. Illustration
   Client: SIK

7. Portrait
   Client: Forbo-Forshaga

8. Comics
   Client: Göteborgs Stad

MARITA ANDERSEN

Vesle-Vollaug
N-2032 Maura
Norway

Tel: +47 63 99 30 69
Fax: +47 63 99 30 15
Email: mari-an@online.no

Works as a visual artist and illustrator

CLAES-GÖRAN ANDERSSON

CGA Information AB
Hara 2155
S-830 23 Hackås
Sweden
Tel: +46 (0)63 181 020/ +46 (0)63 411 54
Fax: +46 (0)63 181 021

I'm a freelance artist working with illustrations and graphic design for the web, multimedia and for printing

PHLAPP

CLAES-GÖRAN ANDERSSON

CGA Information AB
Hara 2155
S-830 23 Hackås
Sweden
Tel: +46 (0)63 181 020/ +46 (0)63 411 54
Fax: +46 (0)63 181 021

I'm a freelance artist working with illustrations and graphic design for the web, multimedia and for printing

ETHEL ÅVALL
• • • • • • • • • • • •

Krokusvägen 4
S-430 91 Hönö
Sweden
Tel/Fax: +46 (0)31 96 61 54

My Education: Master of Fine Arts
Specialité: Illustrations in various style, even graphic design

BJØRN MIKE BOGE

• • • • • • • • • • • •

Sandvigå 24
4007 Stavanger
Norway
Tel: +47 51 52 48 44
Fax: +47 51 56 37 80
Email: bmboge@online.no

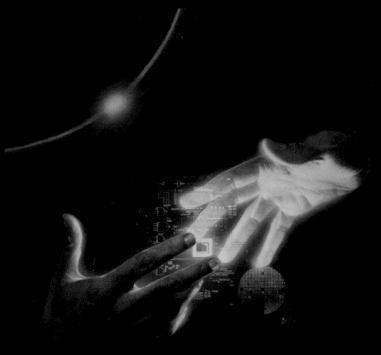

www.triffonarts.com

TRIFFON ARTS

Box 29153
SE-100 52 Stockholm
Sweden
Telephone: +46 (0)8 662 2080
Fax: +46 (0)8 662 2099
info@triffonarts.com

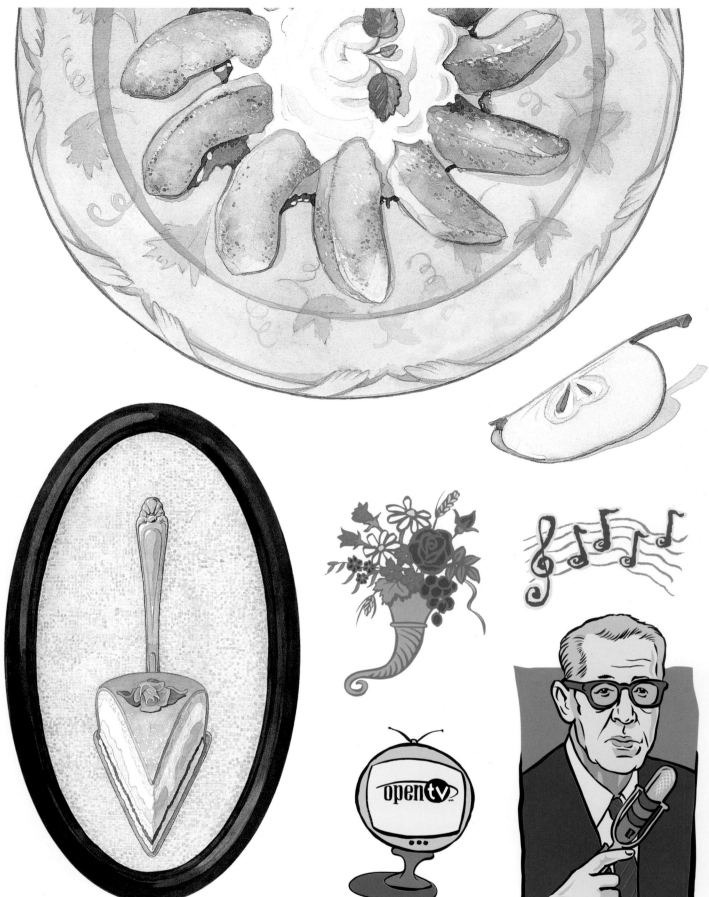

CATHARINA CARLSSON
● ● ● ● ● ● ● ● ● ● ● ●

Arthur & Jag, Tornbergsvägen 1
S-913 35 Holmsund
Sverige
Tel: +46 (0)90 40766
Fax: +46 (0)90 40670
E.Mail: hans.catharina@swipnet.se

BO FURUGREN

Bok, bild & text
Box 15014
S-200 31 Malmö
Sweden
Tel: +46 (0)40 21 35 52

Born 1942
Specialty and interests: animals, biology, science, history

See what this godly sorrow
has produced in you:

What earnestness,
what eagerness
to clear yourselves,
what indignation,
what alarm, what longing,
what concern,
what readiness to
see justice done.

(2 Corinthians 7:11)

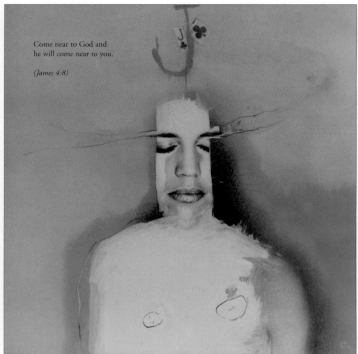

Come near to God and
he will come near to you.

(James 4:8)

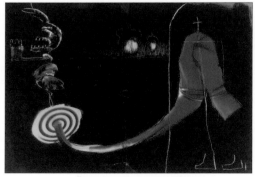

SILJE GRANHAUG
• • • • • • • • • • • •

Hammergata 1
N-0465 Oslo
Norway

Tel: (0047) 22 02 03 91

Freddrik er **POLITIMANN.**

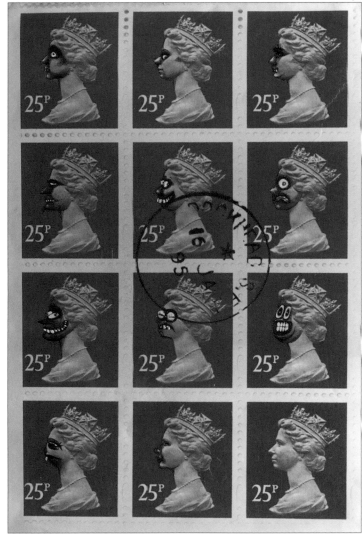

Education:
- 3 years at the National College of Art and Design, Oslo.
- MA Communication Design, Central Saint Martins College of Art and Design, London.

Awards:
- Gold Award and Silver Award in «The Most Beautiul Book of the Year» (Picturebooks).

Experience:
- Art Director in an advertising and design company, Oslo.
- Experience with childrensbooks, bookcovers, magazine illustrations etc.

SILJE GRANHAUG
● ● ● ● ● ● ● ● ● ● ●

Hammergata 1
N-0465 Oslo
Norway

Tel: (0047) 22 02 03 91

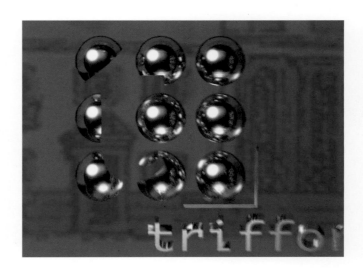

SVANTE SEGELSON

Svante Segelson Illustration
Gotlandsgatan 49
S-116 65 Stockholm
Sweden
Tel: +46 (0)8 642 69 52
Email: svante@segelson.nu
www.segelson.nu

Gör allt som 3D-Produktion innefattar:
Modellering, texturering, animering,
specialeffekter.
Typ av uppdrag: 3D-Animationer till
multimedia eller videoproduktioner

Ola Lindahl

Ynglingavägen 7
S-182 62 Djursholm   Sweden
Tel: +46 8 755 51 60
Fax: +46 8 755 97 31
E-mail: ola.lindahl@mailbox.swipnet.se
Homepage: http://130.244.196.39/~w-56588

Specialization: mild humor
 All kinds of work in Magazines, Books, Web illustrations...
 Animation's for all media: film-video-tv-web-mulimedia-
lasershows....   Even my most hand drawn sketches are
in some stage computer processed.

INGELA JONDELL

Ribegatan 55
S-164 45 Kista
Sweden

Tel: +46 (0)8 751 14 02
Email: ingela@jondell.pp.se

LEIF ÅBJÖRNSSON

• • • • • • • • • • • • •

Åbjörnsson Art AB
Kaptensgatan 11n.b.
SE-114 57 Stockholm
Sweden

Tel: +46 (0)8 662 25 25
Fax: +46 (0)8 660 34 46

sig ofta föder bra mat... Man är helt
enkelt inte hungrig... immin...rites, feta så-
ser och...nna...er sin...ränings-runda eller
sitt jympap... Likson...du...när du...rt dig
lyssna till...roppens signaler, kan skilja den
äkta hungern från stress...en...ter. D...n
rastlösa, stressade...un...ers...ätts o...a l...ta
b...t med en aktiv...te...nå...ot slag. D...t är
en si...al på att kroppen vill h...a...t tillskott
av något, dock inte med nödvändighet mat
eller snac...

Under...ökningar har visat att får kroppen själv...estämma, s...aller den in sig helt
perfekt efter v...d d...n behöver. Det är när
yttre omständig...eter kommer med i spe-
let, som balansen...ubbas.

Man har t ex l...it barn leva i ett oändligt
utbud av mat, d...r...e själv fått välja precis
vad och hur mycket...e vill äta. Det resul-
terade i att...de me...tid...n valde mat som var
allsidig, varierad...ch nä...ringsmässigt helt
perfekt.

H...nger är all...å inte...ara en fråga om
vad k...oppens m...skler behöver för att ut-
rätta s...t arbete. Det h...r också med stäm-
ningsläge...att gö...a. S...ress är ett exempel.
Lycka ett an...at...än...er du dig lycklig är
du faktiskt inte li...a...ungrig, beroende på

CHRISTINA ANDERSSON

* * * * * * * * * *

Barnängsgatan 23E
S-116 41 Stockholm
Sweden
Tel: +46 (0)8 641 32 10
Fax: +46 (0)8 702 93 05
Email: 086413210@telia.com

Clients: Magazines, publishers, advertising agencies
Konstfack University College of Arts Crafts and Design 1993-97
Rhode Island School of Design 1995-96

COMPUTERWORLD

WWW.COMPUTERWORLD.DK · NR. 46A · 18. DECEMBER 1998 · 18. ÅRGANG · LØSSALG: KR. 27,-   DANMARKS IT-AVIS

1998 2000 1999

Dansk e-handel i bund
side 14

IT-folk - en højt skattet mangelvare
side 58

Gates satte kritikerne på plads
side 99

Unix på vej til at gøre comeback
side 106

VIVI

Årsnummer '98

Please take a look at my homepage:

www.vivi.suite.dk

199

SCA

Bang&Olufsen 1998

Public Libraries of Aarhus 1998

Det Talende Værksted

@

For folk der har svært ved at læse

Århus Kommunes Biblioteker

Hovedbiblioteket · Møllegade 1 · 8000 Århus C · Tlf. 87 30 45 00 · www.aakb.bib.dk/tale

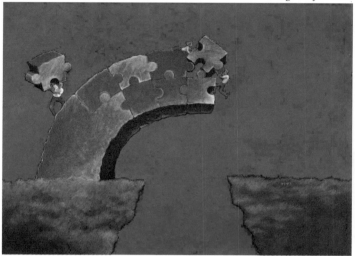

MD Foods 1999

VIVI BARSTED
UNPLUGGED / DIGITAL
ILLUSTRATION

Vestergade No. 1 · Postbox 543 · 8000 Aarhus C · Denmark · Tel: +45 86 13 03 86 · Fax: +45 86 13 09 86 · www.vivi.suite.dk · E-mail: vivi@inet.uni2.dk

Stella East

Doktergarden
N-5730 Ulvik
Norway

Tel: +47 56 52 66 33 • *Fax: +47 56 52 66 61* • *Email: stellast@online.no*

STELLA EAST
"DREAMSTONES"

© SYSTER DIESEL

truly
detestable
summer
festival...

© **SYSTER DIESEL** / **ANNIKA BRYNGELSON**
• • • • • • • • • • • • •

c/o firman, Södra Storgatan 37
S-252 23 Helsingborg
Sweden
Tel: +46 42 18 29 80
Fax: +46 42 18 29 87

GUNNAR FLUSUND

Postboks 9
N-7301 Orkanger
Norway
Tel: +47 (0)72 48 50 06

Født 1963. Utdannelse 3 år videregående skole, grafisk design
Begynte å jobbe med illustrasjon i 1987. Starter eget firma i år.

CHRISTINE GÖHLNER
- - - - - - - - - - - - -

Drömverksta'n
Box 4157
S-400 40 Göteborg
Sweden
Tel: +46 (0)31 29 57 70

Architect, journalist, painting artist & illustrator. Paintings with a lot of details, mostly old houses. Makes Christmas cards, calendars, posters etc.
Architecte, journaliste, artiste-peintre, illustrateur. Peint avec beaucoup de détails, de préférence maisons anciennes. Fait des cartes-postales, calendriers, posters.

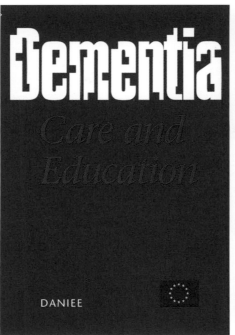

Tjek:
**www.hedegaard -
grafisk.dk**

**Grafisk design og
illustration til bøger, magasiner,
brochurer, plakater m.m.**

ÅSA JÄGERGÅRD
- - - - - - - - - - - - - -

Åsas Firma
Grafisk formgivning & illustration
Box 49
S-824 21 Hudiksvall
Sweden
Tel/Fax: +46 (0)650 133 14

1986-1990 Master of Fine Arts in Graphic Design/Illustration
1991-1994 Art Director
1994- Own Company (Graphic Design/Illustration)

Book Cover
Oil on board
65 x 50cm

Exhibition Piece
Oil on canvas
120 x 90cm

Private Collection
Oil on board
190 x 70cm

FREDRIK JOHRE

Sorgenfrigt. 1
N-0366 Oslo
Norway
Tel: +47 (0,22 59 85 36 / +47 (0)98 84 33 88
Fax: +47 (0)22 59 85 36
Email: Krom@dioksyd.no

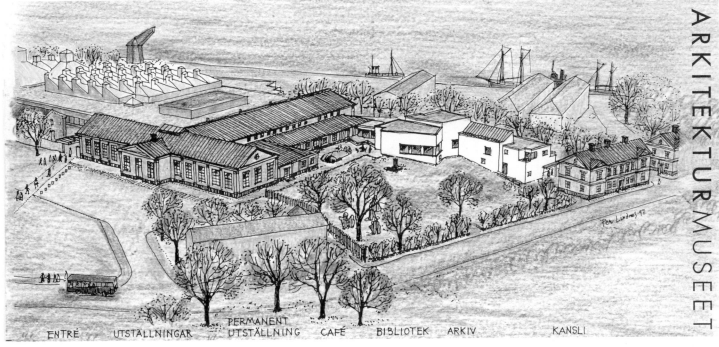

ENTRÉ   UTSTÄLLNINGAR   PERMANENT   CAFÉ   BIBLIOTEK   ARKIV   KANSLI
                            UTSTÄLLNING

ARKITEKTURMUSEET

PER LINDROOS

Nackagatan 29 V
S-116 47 Stockholm
Sweden
Tel/Fax: +46 (0)8 643 80 09 / (0)70 491 19 78

Clients: Statens Fastighetsverk, Spårvägsmuseet, Energimyndigheten
Byggstandardiseringen, Åkers International AB

S.S. POLSTJÄRNAN 11-7-98   Per Lindros

Stockholm 12-7-98

MIKKEL JUUL JENSEN

Bogensegade 10, 5 th
2100 Kbh.Ø
Denmark
Tel/Fax: +45 35 55 05 46
Email: jmj@inet.uni2.dk

Ref: Illustreret Videnskab, Nyhedmagasinet Ingeniøren
I FORM og Komputer for alle

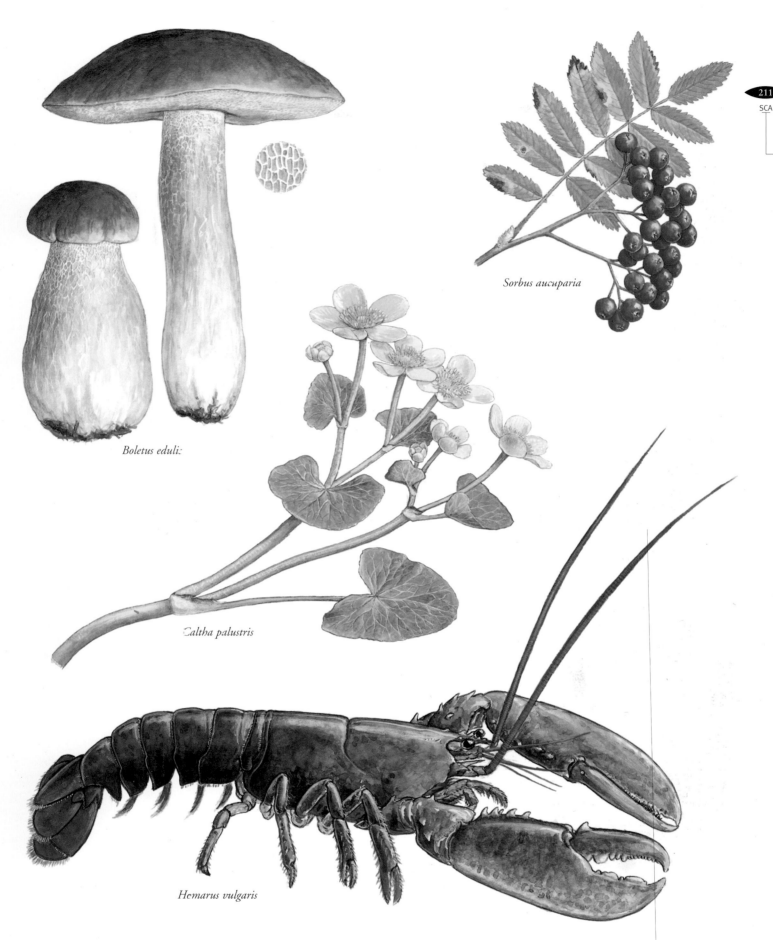

Boletus edulis

Sorbus aucuparia

Caltha palustris

Homarus vulgaris

HERMOD KARLSEN
◆ ◆ ◆ ◆ ◆ ◆ ◆ ◆ ◆ ◆ ◆

Toresmyr 40
N-1634 Gamle Fredrikstad
Norway
Tel: +47 69 34 97 34

Education: Private Art School (2 years) - University of Oslo: Biology, Botany, Chemistry (3 years)
Technics: Water colour, ink pen

BOB KATZENELSON

Tegnestuen De 5
Studiestræde 30, 1
DK-1455 Copenhagen K
Denmark

Tel: +45 33 36 30 18
Fax: +45 33 91 30 18

BO LUNDWALL
● ● ● ● ● ● ● ● ● ●

Hultsfreds Gård
S-577 36 Hultsfred
Sweden
Tel/Fax: +46 (0)495 106 72

Wildlife art, illustration and exhibitions
Techniques: Oil, water colour and lithographs

Birkavägen 14
S-131 40 Nacka
Sweden
Tel: +46 (0)8 718 52 09

Østkystvejen 37
DK-6440 Augustenborg
Denmark

Tel+Fax: +45 7447 4203
E-Mail: meder @ post 5. tele. dk

tegner
peter
meder

the good illustration explains far more than the greatest amount of words

PETER MEDER
. . . .
Østkystvejen 37
DK-6440 Augustenborg
Denmark

Tel+Fax: +45 7447 4203
E-Mail: meder @ post 5. tele. dk

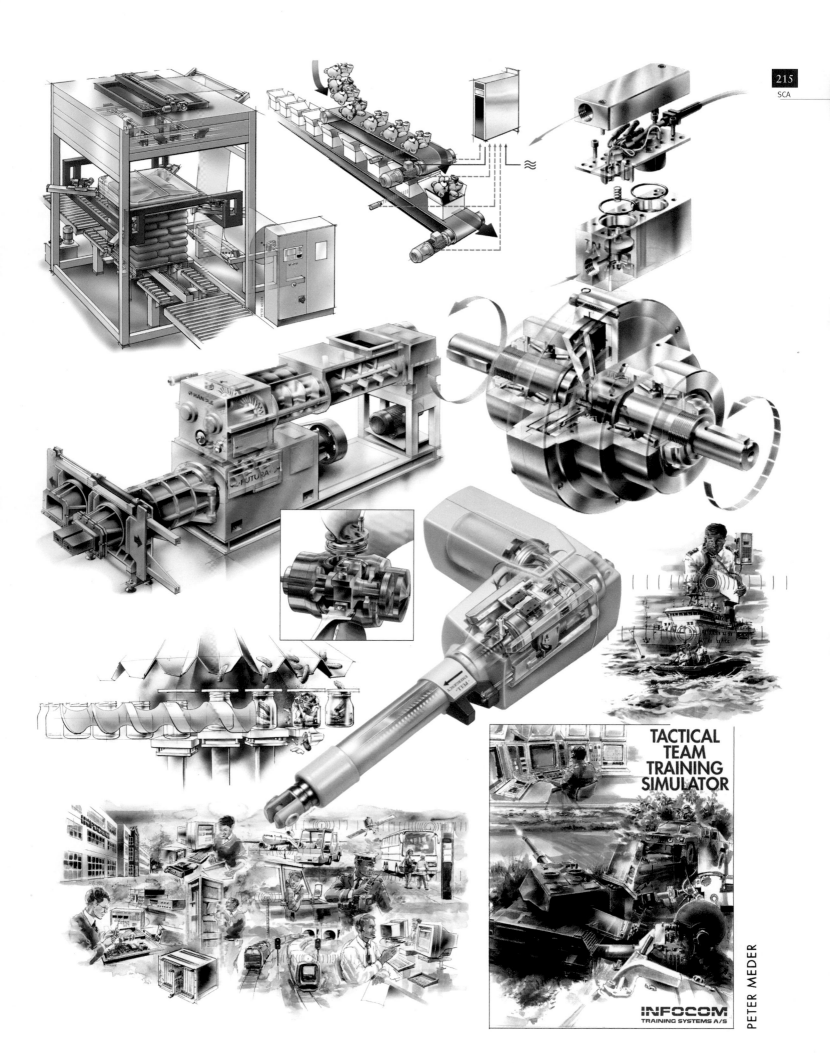

TACTICAL
TEAM
TRAINING
SIMULATOR

INFOCOM
TRAINING SYSTEMS A/S

PETER MEDER

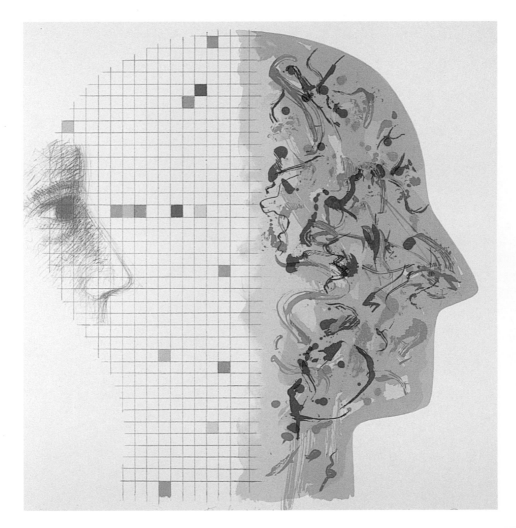

LARS MELANDER

• • • • • • • • • • • •

Ibsengatan 37-39
168 47 Bromma
Sweden
Tel: +46 8 87 16 70
Email: lassemelander@hotmail.com
URL: http://iwelcome.to/larsmelander

ANNE ROOSLIEN

Anne-Teckningar
Kungstensg. 48
S-113 59 Stockholm
Sweden
Tel: +46 (0)8 34 30 10
Fax: +46 (0)8 33 09 55
Mobile: 0708 30 83 93

GRO T. RYKKELID
● ● ● ● ● ● ● ● ● ● ● ●

Vall
N-8170 Engavågen
Norway
Tel: +47 (0) 88 00 24 47
Email: grorykke@online.no

Charlie Norrman

Charlies Bilder AB
Kaptensgatan 11
S-114 57 Stockholm
Sweden

Tel: +46 (0)8 660 27 07
Fax: +46 (0)8 660 27 67

Email: charlies.bilder@swipnet.se

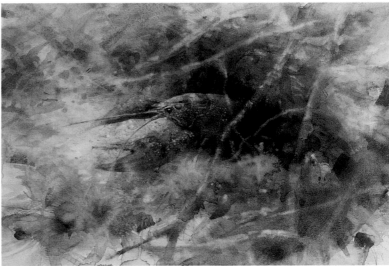

STEFAN HANSSON
• • • • • • • • • • • • •

Siriusgatan 47
S-195 55 Märsta
Sweden
Tel/Fax: +46 (0)8 591 121 03

Several exhibitions in Scandinavia and USA. Books, advertising, museums and galleries
Clients: WWF, NCC, Vattenfall, Watercolor, mixed media, oil and lithography

HARRIET STÅHLBERG
• • • • • • • • • • • •

Harriet Ståhlberg AB
Fersens väg 9
S-211 42 Malmö
Sweden
Tel: +46 (0)40 30 79 79
Fax: +46 (0)40 12 60 59
Email: hs@harrietillustration.com
www.harrietillustration.com

CHRISTER WAHLGREN
·················

Asken Art
Drömminge
S-330 15 Bor. Sweden
Phone and Fax + 46 370-65 07 22
e-mail: asken.art@varnamo.mail.telia.com

CHRISTER WAHLGREN
· · · · · · · · · · · · · · · ·

Asken Art
Drömminge
S-330 15 Bor. Sweden
Phone and Fax + 46 370-65 07 22
e-mail: asken.art@varnamo.mail.telia.com

KAJ WISTBACKA

• • • • • • • • • • • • •

Kaj Wistbacka Illustration och Design
Rörstrandsgatan 8
S-113 40 Stockholm
Sweden
Tel: +46 (0)8 32 24 34

SCA

CECILIA WAXBERG
••••••••••••••

Västergatan 23
S-211 21 Malmö
Sweden
Tel: +46 (0)40 57 97 33
Fax: +46 (0)40 97 96 95
Mobile: +46 (0)708 57 97 30
Email: cecilia@waxberg.m.se
www.waxberg.m.se

SPAIN

ILLUSTRATION
ILUSTRACIÓN

●

Elias, Jordi 74
Gubianas, Jaume 75

JORDI ELIAS
BARCELONA 1964
EDITORIAL,
BOOK PUBLISHING,
ADVERTISING
ILLUSTRATIONS.

SELF-PROMOTIONAL

LA VANGUARDIA, MAGAZINE. (INSOMNIO)

BASSAT, OGILVY & MATHER. (ESADE)

Dr A. Pujadas 2 EB, A2. 08830 Sant Boi. BCN. Spain. Tel-Fax 34. 936307930. www.jelias.com E-mail jelias@idgrup.ibernet.com

ARTIST
Illustrator

jaume gubianas

C/ Anselm Clavé nº 2
08670 NAVÀS (Barcelona)
Tel / Fax: 93 839 07 06
E-mail: gubianas@seker.es
http://bbs.seker.es/~gubianas

UNITED KINGDOM

ILLUSTRATION

●

Anderson, David 82

Arcan, Hamza 78

Baker, Alan 79

Barton, Will 83

Bradley, Gerard 80

Carter, Maureen 81

Collins, Clive 84

Collman, Keith 85

Despotovic, Ivan 86

Dhaimish, Hasan 83

Duszczak, Richard 87

Greenbank, Rachel 88

Holcroft, John 89

Kenyon, Matt 90

Menneer, Neill 91

O'Leary, John 92

Pargeter, Richard 93

Robson, Chris 94

Swift, Gary 95

Waterhouse, Stephen 96

Welbank, Margaret 97

HAMZA ARCAN

1 Salisbury Road
Hove
East Sussex
BN3 3AB
Tel/Fax: +44 (0)1273 205030

ALAN BAKER
● ● ● ● ● ● ● ● ● ● ●

St Michaels
Telscombe Village
Nr Lewes
East Sussex BN7 3HZ
Tel: +44 (0)1273 302333
Fax: +44 (0)1273 300061

I can't boil a tyre or change an egg, but ! can illustrate anything, and get it to you on time

GERARD BRADLEY
• • • • • • • • • • • • •

24 Chichester Road
Belfast
BT15 5EJ
Northern Ireland
Tel: +44 (0)1232 779975

Clients include
Appletree Press • Camden Graphics • Hampden PLC • Housing Executive • DHSS

Maureen Carter

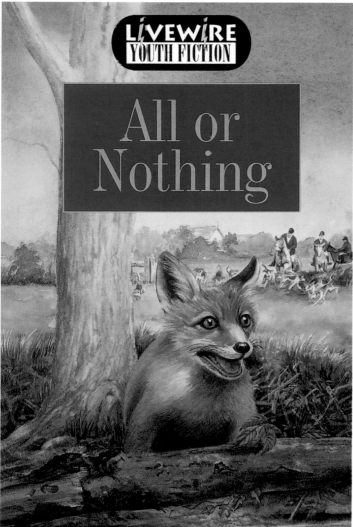

MAUREEN CARTER
• • • • • • • • • • • •

3 Elmfield Close
Weald
Sevenoaks
Kent TN14 6PP
Tel: +44 (0)1732 463474
Fax: +44 (0)1732 463474

Commissions have covered a wide range of work, including black and white, line, and line and wash
Please ring for samples

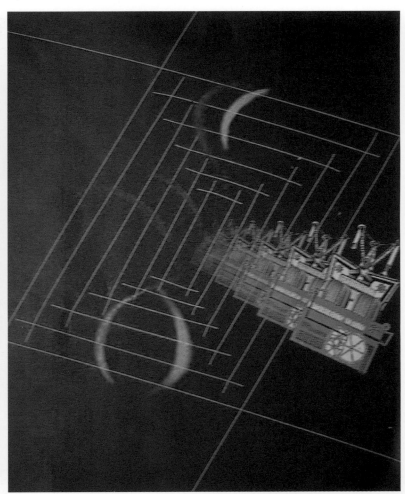

DAVID ANDERSON
• • • • • • • • • • • •

26 Hewitt Street
Hoole
Chester
Cheshire CH2 3JD
Tel: +44 (0)1244 318964

Studied at Liverpool John Moores University
Illustration in pencil, watercolour, acrylics & macintosh computer for magazines, publishing, advertising & greetings cards

WILL BARTON • HASAN DHAIMISH

Two Leaves Design
PO Box 190
Burnley BB10 2GW
Tel: +44 (0)1282 426181 - Fax: +44 (0)1282 426181
Email: will@twoleaves.u-net.com
Web: www.twoleaves.u-net.com

Style, precision, movement, colour, caricature, pen, ink, paint, crayon, airbrush, photo, video
Photoshop, Xpress, Illustrator, Premier • We can do it!

CLIVE COLLINS
••••••••••

251 Highlands Boulevard
Leigh on Sea
Essex
SS9 3TN
Tel/Fax: +44 (0)1702 557205

Clients include: Linguaphone, Readers Digest, Playboy (US), Punch, Mirror Group, ES Magazine
Herald Communications, Shell UK, Samsung Europe, Penguin English

KEITH COLLMAN

Hemel Hempstead
Herts
HP3 9TN
Tel: +44 (0)1442 399234 - Fax: +44 (0)1442 390269
Email: sales@keithcollman.com
Web: www.keithcollman.com

Clients include: F.T, Cespian, Haymarket, Addison Wesley Longman, Heinemann, Ericsson Communication, Reed, Centaur, Director Magazine

85
.

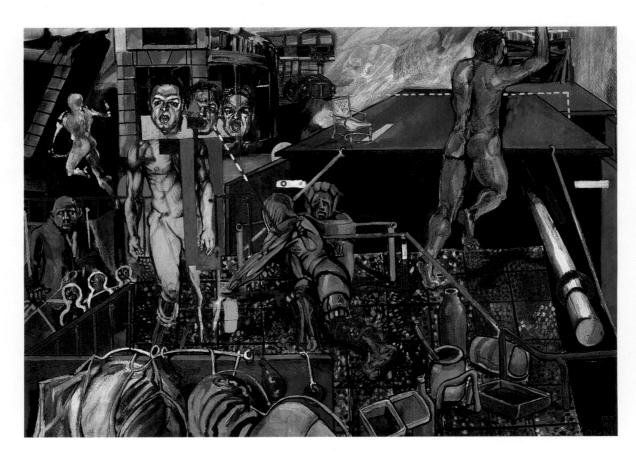

IVAN DESPOTOVIC
. . . .

61 Ravenscourt Road
London W6 0UJ
Tel: +44 (0)20 8741 5522
Fax: +44 (0)20 8741 5522

Illustrator, Animator, Comic Book Artist, Painter

RICHARD DUSZCZAK
• • • • • • • • • • • •

88 Saltergate
Chesterfield
Derbyshire
Tel: +44 (0)1246 209034
Fax: +44 (0)1246 220478

Experienced cartoonist working traditionally or Apple Mac • Ideas man or tight brief - whichever!
Character Creation • Working to make you smile!

RACHEL GREENBANK

•••••••••••

14 Curson Rise
Kendal
Cumbria
LA9 7PN
Tel: +44 (0)1539 726340
Fax: +44 (0)1539 726340

JOHN HOLCROFT
• • • • • • • • • • • • •

The Art Market
27 Old Gloucester Street
London
WC1N 3AF
Tel: +44 (0)20 7209 1123
Fax: +44 (0)20 7209 1129

For further information contact
Philip Reed
at The Art Market

Recent clients include
E.M.A.P • Reed Business Publishing
Centaur Publications • News International

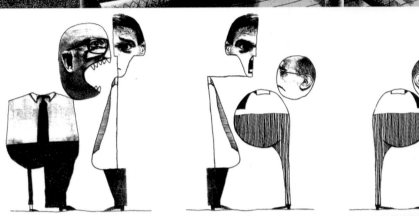

MATT KENYON

19 Malibres Road
Chandlers Ford
Hampshire
SO53 5DS
Tel: +44 (0)1703 265127 - Fax: 0870 056 8345
Mobile: 07005 325705
Email: matthew@kenyons.demon.co.uk

To see more work visit the Kenyon pages at www.kenyons.demon.co.uk

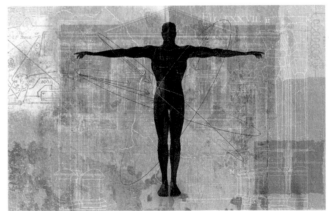

NEILL MENNEER

Belgrave Lodge
Upper Camden Place
Bath BA1 5JA
Tel: +44(0)1225 483151
E-Mail: Photoman@acks.demon.co.uk

*For further examples of my photography and
photo illustrations please see Contact Nos 2-14*

*Clients include: National Westminster Bank,
IBM, Cable and Wireless, LLoyds TSB, Xerox,
Coopers & Lybrand & Future Publishing*

JOHN O'LEARY

16b Charteris Road
Finsbury Park
London N4 3AB
Tel/Fax: +44 (0)20 7272 2521

Recent clients include
What Mortgage • What Investment • Personal Finance • Vertigo • Parents • Longman • Nelson • Frances Lincoln

RICHARD PARGETER

124 Stamford Road
Amblecote
Brierley Hill
West Midlands DY5 2PZ
Tel/Fax: +44 (0)1384 832924
Email: rparg@globalnet.co.uk

CHRIS ROBSON
• • • • • • • • • • •

13 Whatley Road
Clifton
Bristol BS8 2PS
Tel: +44 (0)117 9737 694
Fax: +44 (0)117 9737 694
Mobile: 0797 1379354
Email: cbrobson@aol.com

Clients include: Ford, Volkswagen, Vauxhall, Orange, B.T., Shell, British Airways, Smithkline Beecham, Apple, Bupa, Pedigree Chum, Douwe Egberts and 4:2:2 Videographics

© Fruit Crew

Talk to your plants

Irony....

Monster Bugs

GARY SWIFT

Fieldhouse Studios
8 Hague Park Lane
South Kirkby West Yorkshire
WF9 3SS England
Tel/Fax: +44 (0)1977 646431
www.garyswift.com

Call for a comprehensive sample pack

'St Paul's' for Rowan Fine Art & Editions Ltd

From the 'Twelve Days of Christmas' card for Webb Ivory(Burton)Ltd

One Pink Sari

One pink sari for a pretty girl,
Two dancing women all in a whirl,
Three charmed cobras rising from a basket,
Four fat rubies, in the Rajah's casket,
Five water carriers straight and tall,
Six wicked vultures sitting on the wall,
Seven fierce tigers hiding in the grass,
Eight elephants rolling in a warm mud bath,
Nine green parrots in the coconut tree,
Ten twinkling stars, a-twinkling at me!

Ann Marie Linden

For the poetry book 'Whizz Bang Orang-Utan' by Oxford University Press

*From the Children's book
'The Bird Market' by Stephen Waterhouse*

STEPHEN WATERHOUSE
· · · · · · · · · · · · · · · ·

*2a Norwood Grove
Birkenshaw - Bradford
West Yorkshire BD11 2NP
Tel: +44 (0)1274 877111 - Fax: +44 (0)1274 877111
Mobile: 07971 347856
Minifolio: www.contact-uk.com/stephenwaterhouse*

Illustration for print & design, children's and general publishing

*Clients:
Cambridge University Press,
Harper Collins Books,
Popshots Ltd,
Radio Times*

MARGARET WELBANK

●●●●●●●●●●●●

88b Mansfield Road
London
NW3 2HX
Tel: +44 (0)20 7267 8658
Fax: +44 (0)20 7267 8658

Illustration and cartoons, particularly educational and technical subjects
Clients include: Channel 4, Top Santé, OUP, WWF-UK, Barnet Council, BP

AOI

ASSOCIATION OF ILLUSTRATORS

UNITED KINGDOM

ADVERTISING
Bailey, Veronica .20
Bliss, Stephen .21
Brownfield, Mick .22
Craste, Marc 17
Ellis, Max 23
Harrison, Matilda 24
Hunt, Philip .18
Johnson, Adrian .22
Khoo, Chuan .25
Lang, Alison .26
Love, Frank .27
Mackie, Clare .28
Marsh, James .29
Pollock, Ian .30
Potter, Ashley .19
Spilsbury, Simon .31
Till, Peter .32
Webster, David .33

CHILDREN'S BOOKS
Balit, Christina .38
Baran, Barbara .39
Baran, Zafer .39
Bartram, Simon .40
Becker, Greg .42
Boni, Simoni .48
Fitzsimons, Cecilia .43
Flavin, Teresa .46
Gower, Teri .47
Gudynas, Bernard .45
Gudynas, Peter .44
Harrison, Matilda .41
Hartas, Leo .48
Mackie, Clare .50
Mayer, Danuta .49
Monks, Lydia .51
Pudles, Daniel .52
Pyle, Liz .53
Rayner, Olivia .54
Stephens, Helen .55
Warner, Peter .56, 57
Willey, Bee .37
Wyatt, David .48

EDITORIAL
Adler, Alan .74
Bailey, Veronica .75
Baran, Barbara .76, 77
Baran, Zafer .76, 77
Bridge, Andy .62
Briers, Stuart .70
Butcher, Bill .78
Bylo, Andrew .71
Calder, Jill .80, 81
Climpson, Sue .68
Combi, Linda .79
Corr, Christopher .62
Deboo, Cyrus .82
Disley, Philip .83
Djordjevic, Jovan .84, 85
Ellis, Max .69
Ford, Jason .60, 61
Goodal, Jasper .86
Gowdy, Carolyn .65
Graff, Adam .87
Grandfield, Geoff .64
Hardcastle, Nick .88
Hassall, Jo .89
Hauff, Kevin .90
Hudson, Frazer .91
Kambayashi, Satoshi .92, 93
Knock, Peter .94
Lee, Sean .64
Löhlein, Henning .95
Love, Frank .67
Lush, Debbie .63
Magill, Anne .96
Marsh, James .97
McBeth, Glen .98
McGowan, Shane .99
McSweeney, Tony .100
Newington, Kate .101
O'Keefe, Kevin .66
Pellatt, Ali .72
Robson, Chris .102
Sanderson, Bill .65
Selby, Andrew .103
Sobr, Penny .104
Steinberg, Anna .73
Tang, Kam .63
Till, Peter .105

GENERAL BOOKS
Dimitranova, Nelly .109
Grandfield, Geoff .110, 111
Gudynas, Peter .108
Hilling, Lesley .112
Horse, Harry .113
Jones, Peter Simon .114
Magill, Anne .115
Marsh, James .116
Mason, Daren .117
Perkins, Sarah .118, 119
Pollock, Ian .120
Tolford, Nancy .121
Van Loon, Borin .122
Woods, Rosemary .123

INFORMATION
Bimrose, Paul .127
Glover, Jeremy .129
Harland, Angela .126
Hawke, Jean .140
Holmes, Mark .128
Jacks, Christopher .129
Jennings, Anne Louise .130
Kenyon, Elaine .131
Latimer, Jonathan .132
Miller, Alastair .133
Milne, Annabel .141
Orr, Chris .142
Palmer, Stephen .134
Rowbottom, Stuart .135
Smith, William .136
Turner, Brian .137
Wilcock, Martin .138
Wood, Andrew .139

PRINT & DESIGN
Allen, Ivan .148
Baran, Barbara .149
Baran, Zafer .149
Bliss, Stephen .150
Burke, Kirsten Leonora .151
Calder, Jill .152
Clark, Michael .153
Coleman, Sarah .154
Combi, Linda .155
Dimitranova, Nelly .156
Gomez, Elena .157
Gunson, Christopher .158
Hamilton, Jon D .159
Harrison, Matilda .147
Hayward, Sara .160
Hughes, Ciaran .161
Jobling, Curtis .162
Kambayashi, Satoshi .163
Mackie, Clare .166
Magill, Anne .167
Marsh, James .168
Milner, Maggy .169
Mitchell, Aileen .170
Murray, Ian .171
Morgan-Jones, Tom .164
Perkins, Sarah .172
Pinn, Ingram .173
Pollock, Ian .174
Powis, Paul .175
Sheehy, Michael .176
Terry, Michael .177
Till, Peter .178
Walker, Russell .179
Wormell, Christopher .165

STUDENT
Calvert, Richard .185
Cusick, Jonathan .186 - 188
Dunbar, Colin .203
Etheridge, Tim .189
Fraser-Coombe, Warwick .190
Hearn, Samuel .191
Johnson, Richard .192
Lockwood, Sarah .193
Mair, David .203
Matsushita, Saeko .194
Myers, Richard .204
Rowbottom, Stuart .203
Samuels, Graham .204
Tadd, Nikki .204
Tatcheva, Eva .195
Taylor, Nicola .205
Thomas, Laura Madeleine .205
Torseter, Oyvind .205
Uthaiah, Chitra .196
Van Wyk, Rupert .206
Wainwright, Neil .197
Ward, Mark .198
Waterhouse, Stephen .182 - 184
West, Annette .199
Williams, Olivia .200
Willshaw, Sarah .206
Wilson, Sam .201
Wiseman, Helen .206
Wyatt, Paula .202

UNPUBLISHED
Black, Sarah .212
Bliss, Stephen .213
Borden, Nicholas .214
Bramman, Michael .215
Breeden, Neil .216
Brook, Hazel Natasha .217
Buckley, Harriet .218
Burke, Karen .219
Calder, Jill .210, 211
Carroll, Steven .220
Carruthers, Grant .221
Davies, Joanne .224, 225
Davies, Peter .223
Davies, Simon John .222
Dewar, Nick .226
Donohoe, Heidi .227
Feneziani, Serena .228
Garner, Ged .229
Gomez, Elena .230
Green, Nicolette .231
Grimwood, Brian .232
Grover, Sally .233
Harris, Andrew .234
Heskins, Valerie .236
Joyce, Sophie .237
Lang, Alison .238
Lees, Stewart .239
Love, Frank .240, 241
Lewis, Jan .242
Magill, Anne .243
McDonald, Brigitte .244
McGowan, Shane .245
Mellor, Belle .246
Mina, Rosalyn .247
Parfitt, George .248
Piero (Hernan Pierini) .235
Please, Sophia .249
Pollock, Ian .250
Powis, Paul .251
Richardson, Matthew .252, 253
Ryder, Johanne .254
Till, Peter .255
Wakefield, Helen .256
Young, Alan .257

judges

Henry Rossiter **art director** Ogilvy Mather
Sally Bide **head of art buying** BMP DDB
Jim Landen **creative director** Barkers Advertising
David Hughes **illustrator**

★ award winner: *The AOI*
Kall Kwik Illustrator Award
★ Advertising section winner

marc craste

a.k.a Pizazz Ltd
30 Berwick Street
Soho
London W1V 3RF

t. 0171 434 3581
f. 0171 437 2309
email. info@studioaka.co.uk

GB

title
Orange Reception
medium
Acrylics on card
purpose of work
Advertising
brief
To show that
Orange are
installing more
transmitters

commissioned by
Steve Little/Tim
Robertson
company
WCRS
client
Orange
agent
a.k.a Pizazz Ltd
30 Berwick Street
London W1V 3AF
t. 0171 434 3581

philip hunt

a.k.a. Pizazz Ltd
30 Berwick Street
Soho
London W1V 3RF
t. 0171 434 3581
f. 0171 437 2309
email. philip@studioaka.co.uk

title
Hills

medium
Mixed media /
Digital

purpose of work
Advertising

brief
To show that
Orange works,
wherever you are

commissioned by
Steve Little/Tim
Robertson

company
WCRS

client
Orange

agent
a.k.a. Pizazz Ltd
30 Berwick Street
London W1V 3AF
t. 0171 434 3581

ashley potter

The Dairy
5-7 Marischal Road
London
SE13 5LE

t. 0181 297 2212
f. 0181 297 2212

Original Design Illustration

Broadcast Image

title
Words
medium
Mixed
purpose of work
Design for
television
commercial

brief
Depict script in a
visually arresting
and witty fashion
commissioned by
a.k.a. Pizazz Ltd
client
Orange

veronica bailey

188 Langham Road
Turnpike Lane
London
N15 3NB

t. 0181 888 0606
f. 0181 374 1891

20
GB

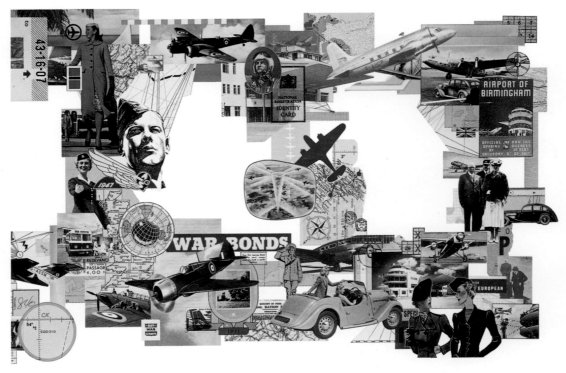

title
History of
Birmingham Airport

medium
Collage

purpose of work
Mural for airport
visitors centre

brief
Illustrate the
history of
Birmingham airport
from 1939 to the
year 2000

commissioned by
Stuart Richie

company
Cole Hansle

client
Birmingham Airport

agent
Debut Art
30 Tottenham
Street, London
W1 9PN
t. 0171 636 1064

stephen bliss

Flat 4
110 Edith Grove
London
SW10 0NH

t. 0171 352 7686
f. 0171 376 8727

21
GB

title
I Drink Therefore I
Am
medium
Acrylic on Billboard
purpose of work
Advertising

brief
To advertise the
fun aspects of
drinking Foster's
Ice beer and to
paint directly onto
the billboard
commissioned by
Paul Tully
company
Paul Tully & Co
client
Foster's Ice for
Scottish Courage

mick brownfield

22
GB

24 Richmond Hill
Richmond
Surrey TW10 6QX

t. 0181 940 1303
f. 0181 332 1451

title
Four Over Par
medium
Press/posters/
postcards/t-shirts
purpose of work
Advertising the
Murphy's Irish
Open 1997

brief
Promote brand and
Irish Open;
support TV
campaign;
challenge target's
preconception
about golf and
Murphy's
commissioned by
Fleur Jerome
company
Bartle Bogle
Hegarty
client
Murphy's Brewery,
Ireland

adrian johnson

5 Ridley Road
London
NW10 5UB

t. 0181 965 8918
f. 0181 965 8918
mobile. 0958 670750

title
Hedgehog
medium
Train panels and
press
purpose of work
To encourage
people to make a
humorous
connection
between Frisk and
their enhanced
personal
performance

brief
Frisk sharpens you
up
commissioned by
Fiona Curzon
company
Bartle Bogle
Hegarty
client
Perfetti

max ellis

See Agent

23
GB

title
Future Bitch

medium
Digital montage

purpose of work
Advertising posters,
flyers, installation

brief
Come up with a
futuristic trans-
sexual future bitch
image for a 35ft
installation and
posters for club by
Ministry of Sound

commissioned by
Will Harvey

company/client
Ministry of Sound

agent
Illustration
1 Vicarage Crescent
Clapham
London SW11 3LP
t. 0171 228 8882

title	**brief**	**agent**
IBM Flying Sheep	"We weren't	Arena
medium	sleeping, only	144 Royal College
Acrylics	dreaming". play	Street
	on the idea of	Camden
purpose of work	counting sheep	London
Advertising	**commissioned by**	NW1 oTA
Campaign for	Christina Hufgard	t. 0171 267 9661
Germany		
	company	
	Olgilvy & Mather	
	Frankfurt	

chuan khoo

27 Whitmore Street
Maidstone
Kent
ME16 8JX

t. 01622 721 987
f. 01622 721 987

title
Return to Nursing
medium
Acrylic and
gouache
purpose of work
Poster
advertisement and
flyer

brief
Produce attractive
illustration aimed
at encouraging
former health
workers and nurses
to attend refresher
courses in order to
return to the
nursing profession
commissioned by
Henry Giddings
company/client
Middlesex
University

alison lang

Suite 7
24 Warwick Road
London
SW5 9UD

t. 0171 598 1037
f. 0171 598 1037

26

GB

title
Career on the
Circle Line

medium
Scraperboard

purpose of work
To appear on tube
station posters
promoting Kall
Kwik

brief
To show
exasperated man
working in circles

commission by
Andy Bull

company
Three Blind Mice

client
Kall Kwik

frank love

The Dairy
5-7 Marischal Road
London
SE13 5LE

t. 0181 297 2212
f. 0181 297 2212

title
Cat Man's Tale

medium
Mixed media

purpose of work
Theatre poster /
postcard /
pamphlet

brief
Portray central
character: a priest
who loses faith and
who is redeemed
through lion taming

commissioned by
Simon Williams

company
Tangerine Ltd

client
Opera Circus

agent
Eastwing
98 Columbia Road
London
E2 7QB
t. 0171 613 5580

clare mackie

21a Ursula Street
London
SW11 3DW

t. 0171 223 8649
f. 0171 223 4119

28
GB

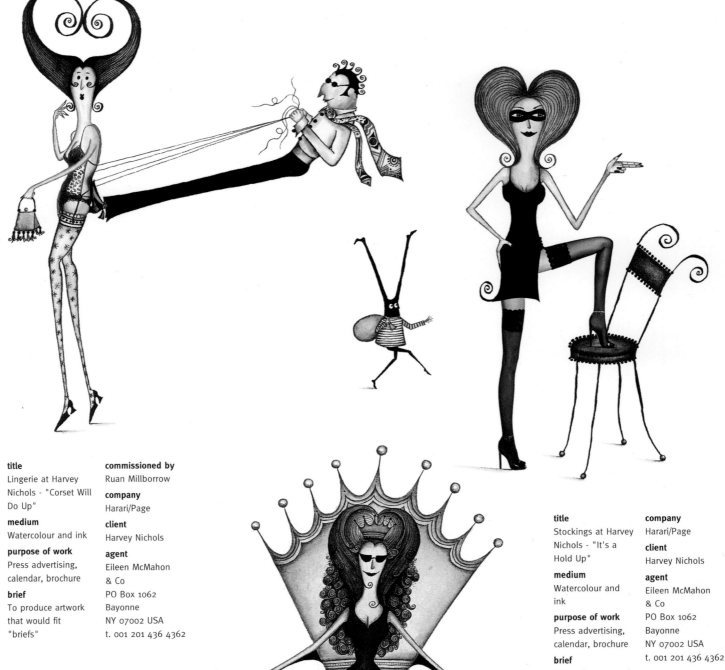

title
Lingerie at Harvey
Nichols - "Corset Will
Do Up"

medium
Watercolour and ink

purpose of work
Press advertising,
calendar, brochure

brief
To produce artwork
that would fit
"briefs"

commissioned by
Ruan Millborrow

company
Harari/Page

client
Harvey Nichols

agent
Eileen McMahon
& Co
PO Box 1062
Bayonne
NY 07002 USA
t. 001 201 436 4362

title
Stockings at Harvey
Nichols - "It's a
Hold Up"

medium
Watercolour and
ink

purpose of work
Press advertising,
calendar, brochure

brief
To produce artwork
for ad with gap left
for photomontage

commissioned by
Ruan Millborrow

company
Harari/Page

client
Harvey Nichols

agent
Eileen McMahon
& Co
PO Box 1062
Bayonne
NY 07002 USA
t. 001 201 436 4362

title
Windsor Royal
Station Shopping
Centre

medium
Watercolour and ink

purpose of work
Brochures,
haordings,
magazines, ads, etc

brief
To produce an
image that was
vaguely royal and all
about shopping

commissioned by
Mary Portas

company
Yellow door

client
Windsor Royal
Station

agent
Eileen McMahon
& Co
PO Box 1062
Bayonne
NY 07002 USA
t. 001 201 436 4362

james marsh

21 Elms Road
London
SW4 9ER

t. 0171 622 9530
f. 0171 498 6851

GB

title
The Barber of
Saville
medium
Acrylic on canvas
board
purpose of work
Advertisement for
insurance company

brief
To illustrate copy
'Mozart would have
been a terrible
barber'
commissioned by
Alicia Tyson
company
ACC, Canada
client
Starr Excess

ian pollock

171 Bond Street
Macclesfield
Cheshire
SK11 6RE

t. 01625 426205
f. 01625 261390

30
GB

title
Now Worse than
Ever
medium
Watercolour ink
and gouache
purpose of work
Poster

brief
Poster for the
London Dungeon
commissioned by
Roger Sealey
company
DMB&B
agent
The Inkshed
98 Columbia Road
London
E2 7QB
t. 0171 613 2323

simon spilsbury

36 Wellington
Street
London
WC2

t. 0171 836 1090
f. 0171 836 1090

31

GB

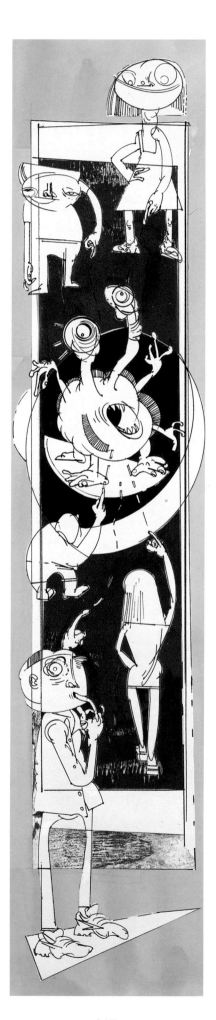

title
Five Children and It
medium
Ink and Acrylic

purpose of work
To persuade
children to read
more through
intrigue

brief
To illustrate banner
poster on 'Five
Children and It'

commissioned by
Duncan Moore

company
Moore Lowenhoff

peter till

11 Berkeley Road
London
N8 8RU

t. 0181 341 0497
f. 0181 341 0497

title
Och!
medium
Pen, ink and
watercolour
purpose of work
Press and poster
ad
brief
To illustrate an
anecdote about the
Macallan
commissioned by
Jim Downie
company
Faulds Advertising
client
Macallan

title
Nae Fish
medium
Pen, ink and
watercolour
purpose of work
Press and poster
ad
brief
I was given an
anecdote about the
Macallan
commissioned by
Jim Downie
company
Faulds Advertising
client
Macallan

david webster

60 Parfett Street
London
E1 1JR

t. 0171 375 1440
f. 0171 375 1440

GB

title
Daihatsu 'The
Grand Move'

medium
Ink

purpose of work
Advertise the new
Daihatsu 'Move'

brief
To produce
drawings for five
different 96 sheet
billboard
advertisements /
national press ads.
The billboard
advertisements
were printed in
fluorescent inks

commissioned by
Banks Hoggins
O'Shea

client
Daihatsu

agent
Artbank
International
8 Woodcroft
Avenue
London
t. 0181 906 2288

judges

Claire Bond **art director** Hodder Children's Books
Ann Glenn **children's art director** MacMillan Children's Books
Laura Cecil **literary agent**
Allan Drummond **illustrator**
Shireen Nathoo **director** Shireen Nathoo Design

children's books

★ winner in children's book section
★ winner: *Transworld Children's Book Award*

bee willey

6 Beck Road
London
E8 4RE

t. 0181 986 5933

37

GB

title
The Pear Tree

medium
Mixed media, ink, pencil, oil pastel

purpose of work
To depict the life around the pear tree throughout the seasons

brief
May: to depict the joys for Spring blossom
August: to depict sultry heat in English Summer

commissioned by
Alison Green

company/client
Macmillan

agents
(Children's Books)
Caroline Walsh / David Higham
5-8 Lower John Street
W1
0171 437 7888
(General Illustration)
Jacquie Figgis
Eel Brook Studios
125 Moore Park Road
SW6 4PS
t. 0171 610 9933

christina balit

Pym Lodge
Soles Hill Road
Shottenden
Kent
CT4 8JU

t. 01227 730029
f. 01227 730029

38
GB

title
Zoo in the Sky
(Series of 3)

medium
Watercolour and
gouache and silver
foil

purpose of work
To illustrate full
children's book
"Zoo in the Sky"

brief
To illustrate the
animal
constellations in
the night sky - non-
astrological and
astrological for a 3-
8 age group. A
very accurate guide
that can be held
up.

commissioned by
Frances Lincoln

zafer & barbara baran

47 Kings Road
Richmond
Surrey
TW10 6EG

t. 0181 948 3050
f. 0181 948 3050

title
The Diversity of
Life
medium
Liquid watercolour
and ink
purpose of work
Children's book
illustration

brief
To illustrate piece
on bio-diversity
published in
'Anthology for the
Earth'
commissioned by
Jim Bunker
company/client
Walker Books

title
Pinocchio

medium
Acrylics

purpose of work
Illustrated picture
book

brief
To illustrate
Pinocchio, keeping
to the original
Italian text

commissioned by
Jane Thomas

company
Dorling Kindersley
Children's Fiction

agent
Arena
144 Royal College
Street
Camden
London
NW1 0TA
t. 0171 267 9661

title
Bisky Bats and
Pussy Cats

medium
Acrylics

brief
To illustrate the
nonsense rhymes
and poetry of
Edward Lear

commissioned by
Sarah Odedina

company
Bloomsbury
Children's Books

agent
Arena
144 Royal College
Street
Camden
London
NW1 0TA
t. 0171 267 9661

greg becker

41 Whateley Road
East Dulwich
London
SE22 9DE

t. 0181 693 6120
f. 0181 693 6120

42
GB

title
1. Hook and Smee
2. The Lost Boys
3. Mr Darling's New
   Home

medium
Acrylic paint

purpose of work
Book Illustration

brief
To provide five full
pages and ten
smaller colour
pictures for 'Peter
Pan' by JM Barrie

commissioned by
Amy McKay

company
Antique Collectors
Club Ltd

cecilia fitzsimons

Woodstock Lodge
25 Hazelgrove
Clanfield
Nr Waterlooville
Hants PO8 oLE

t. 01705 597076
f. 01705 597076
e-mail. ceciliafitzsimons@compuserve.com

GB

title	**commissioned by**
Rainforest bugs	David West
medium	**company**
Watercolour and	David West
gouache	Children's Books
purpose of work	**agency**
Double page	Wildlife Art
spread for giant	Studio 16,
bugs book	Muspole Workshops
brief	25-27 Muspole
Very realistic.	Street
South American	Norwich
jungle scene,	NR3 1DJ
detailed insects,	
not "picked out" -	
blend as holistic	
scene. Research all	
species	

peter gudynas

Zap Art
89 Hazelwell Crescent
Stirchley
Birmingham
B30 2QE

t. 0121 459 0080
f. 0121 459 0080
e-mail. peter@zapart.demon.co.uk

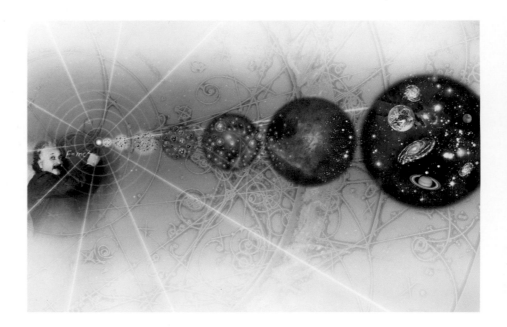

title
The Big Bang
Echoes of Creation
The Search for ET

medium
Digital

purpose of work
Illustrations for the
Kingfisher Book of
Space, an
educational
children's book and
for anyone who has
ever looked up in
wonder at the night
sky and imagined
what lies beyond
planet Earth

brief
Illustrating themes
concerned with
space and physics,
the big bang, the
creation of the
universe, and the
search for extra-
terrestrial lifeforms

commissioned by
Suè Aldworth and
Clive Wilson

company/client
Kingfisher
Publications plc

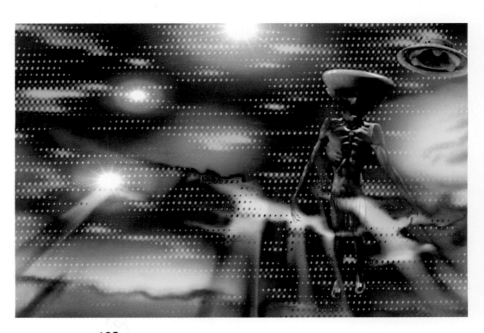

bernard gudynas

Zap Art
Studio 4
59 Nevill Road
Stoke Newington
London N16 8SW

t. 0171 923 3618
f. 0171 249 2775
email: bernie@zapart.demon.co.uk

45

GB

title
Using Space
Impossible
Questions
Black Holes

medium
Digital

purpose of work
Illustrations for the
Kingfisher Book of
Space, an
educational
children's book and
for anyone who has
ever looked up in
wonder at the night
sky and imagined
what lies beyond
planet Earth

brief
To show the
different types of
satellites and their

orbits and to
explain some of
their uses

Why are we here?
What lies beyond
the Universe?
What were the
circumstances that
made life and the
universe possible?

To explain the
theory of black
holes digitally re-
using Tenniel's
Alice and the white
rabbit

commissioned by
Sue Aldworth and
Clive Wilson

company/client
Kingfisher
Publications plc

131

CHILDREN'S BOOKS

teresa flavin

WASPS Studios
3rd Floor,
22 King Street
Glasgow
G1 5QP

t. 0141 552 2251
f. 0141 552 2251

46
GB

title
The Old Cotton
Blues
medium
Gouache
purpose of work
Children's picture
book
brief
Illustration for a
story set in New
York City

commissioned by
Ann Bobco
company
McElderry Books /
Simon & Schuster
agency
Publishers'
Graphics (North
America only)
251 Greenwood
Avenue
Bethel,
CT 06801-2400
USA

teri gower

Little Talland
Firle
East Sussex
BN8 6NT

t. 01273 858193
f. 01273 858193
Internet contact-uk.com/terigower

title	commissioned by
Sometimes I am Naughty	Brimax
medium	**agent**
Line and wash	Malcolm Sherman
purpose of work	Little Talland
Children's book	Firle
brief	East Sussex
Completely open brief requiring fun, bright, child friendly illustrations	BN8 6NT

david wyatt

48

GB

St Caverne
South Zeal
Okehampton
Devon
EX20 2JP

t. 01837 840710

title
General
Beauregard's
Haunted House
medium
Magazine and
eventually to book
purpose of work
Haunted World
Pages of Spine
Chiller Magazine

brief
To visualise and
illustrate from text
supplied - must
have a spooky
atmosphere and fit
with style of
magazine
commissioned by
Art Director : Bob
Hook; Art Editor :
Chantal Newell
Designer : Jessica
Watts

company
Eaglemoss
Publications
agent
Sarah Brown
10 The Avenue
Ealing, London
W13 8PH
t. 0181 998 0390

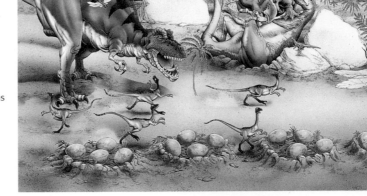

simoni boni

via Montebello 39
50123 Florence
Italy

t. 0039 552 302816

title
Dinosaurs
medium
Magazine and book
purpose of work
Puzzle Strand of
spine chiller
magazine

brief
To illustrate text as
supplied in a
dramatic interesting
manner
commissioned by
Art Director : Bob
Hook
Art Editor : Chantal
Newell
Designer : Andy
Archer

company
Eaglemoss
Publications
agent
Virgil Pomfret
Agency
25 Sispara Gardens
London
t. 0181 785 6167

leo hartas

41 Lincoln Street
Brighton
East Sussex
BN2 2UG

t. 01273 388172

title
Under the Sea
medium
Magazine and
eventually to book
purpose of work
Puzzle Strand of
Spine Chiller
Magazine

brief
To illustrate within
the style of the
magazine
commissioned by
Art Director : Bob
Hook
Art Editor : Chantal
Newell

company
Eaglemoss
Publications

danuta mayer

51 Sunnyhill Road
London
SW16 2UG

t. 0181 677 7043

title
Rikki-tikki-tavi

medium
Gouache

purpose of work
Children's book
illustrations

brief
To illustrate new
pocket-sized
edition of Rudyard
Kipling's classic,
'Rikki-tikki-tavi'

commissioned by
Amelia Edwards

company/client
Walker Books

clare mackie

21a Ursula Street
London
SW11 3DW

t. 0171 223 8649
f. 0171 223 4119

50
GB

title
Michael Rosen's
Book of Nonsense -
Cover

medium
Watercolour and
ink

purpose of work
Children's Book

brief
To illustrate the
poetry of Michael
Rosen

commissioned by
Wendy Knowles

company/client
Macdonad Young
Books

title
Michael Rosen's
Book of Nonsense -
"More, More,
More"

medium
Watercolour and
ink

purpose of work
Children's Book

brief
To illustrate the
poetry of Michael
Rosen

commissioned by
Wendy Knowles

company/client
Macdonad Young
Books

title
Michael Rosen's
Book of Nonsense -
"The Bus"

medium
Watercolour and
ink

purpose of work
Children's Book

brief
To illustrate the
poetry of Michael
Rosen

commissioned by
Wendy Knowles

company/client
Macdonad Young
Books

lydia monks

64 Frankfurt Road
Herne Hill
London
SE24 9NY

t. 0171 274 4158
f. 0171 274 4158

GB

title
Bad Bad Cats

medium
Mixed

purpose of work
Illustrate a book of
poems

brief
To illustrate a book
of poems by Roger
McGough in black
and white

commissioned by
Ronnie Fairweather

company
Puffin Books

agent
Hilary Delamere /
The Agency
24 Pottery Land
London
W11 4LZ
t. 0171 727 1346

daniel pudles

8 Herschell Road
London
SE23 1EG

t. 0181 699 8540
f. 0181 699 8540

52
GB

title
Twice my size

medium
Print from woodcut

purpose of work
A series of 12
illustrations for a
picture book

brief
To illustrate a
poem by Adrian
Mitchell

commissioned by
Sarah Odedina

company
Bloomsbury
Children's Books

liz pyle

29 London Fields
East Side
London
E8 3SA

t. 0171 275 7973
f. 0171 275 7973

53
GB

title
Somewhere Out
There

medium
Pastel

purpose of work
Children's Book

brief
To illustrate the
children's book
'Somewhere Out
There' by Jonathan
Meres

commissioned by
Caroline Roberts

company
Hutchinson's
Children's Books

olivia rayner

54

GB

29 Collett Road
London
SE16 4DJ

t. 07071 226 296
pager. 04325 239493

title
North American
Myths and Legends
medium
Acrylics and mixed
media
purpose of work
Children's Book:
Storybook/Anthrop
ological
brief
To illustrate a
native American
myth: "Black Bird,
Bright Skies"

helen stephens

Flat 2
295 King Street
Hammersmith
London
W6 9NH

t. 0181 563 8919
f. 0181 563 8919

55
GB

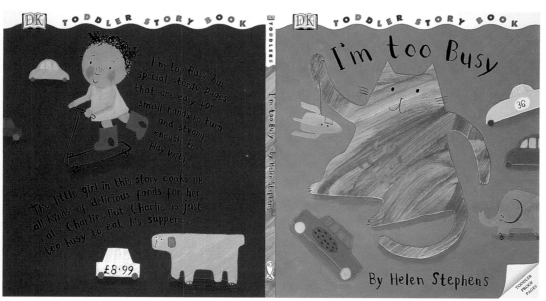

title
I'm Too Busy
medium
Acrylic
purpose of work
Children's Book

brief
To write and
illustrate a
children's book for
Dorling Kindersley's
Toddler series
commissioned by
Fiona Macmillan
company/client
Dorling Kindersley,
Children's Fiction

peter warner

Peter Warner's Studio
Hillside Road
Tatsfield
Kent
TN16 2NH

t. 01959 577270
f. 01959 541414
mobile. 0958 531538
www.contact-uk.com/Peter Warner

title
Swan in the Swin

medium
Watercolour

purpose of work
Book Jacket design
for one of a series
of children's books

brief
Emphasis is on
animal appeal and
drama. The direct,
loose, spontaneous
approach was
devised for the
series, now very
successful.
Preparatory
drawings are
minimal.

commissioned by
Claire Sutton

company
Hodder Children's
Books

peter warner

Peter Warner's Studio
Hillside Road
Tatsfield
Kent
TN16 2NH

t. 01959 577270
f. 01959 541414
mobile. 0958 531538
www.contact-uk.com/Peter Warner

57

GB

title
Lion by the Lake
medium
Watercolour
purpose of work
Book Jacket design
for one of a series
of children's books

brief
Emphasis is on
animal appeal and
drama. The direct,
loose, spontaneous
approach was
devised for the
series, now very
successful.
Preparatory
drawings are
minimal.
commissioned by
Claire Sutton

company
Hodder Children's
Books

judges

Justin Colby **senior designer** FHM

Wayne Ford **art director** Observer Life Magazine

Ian Whadcock **illustrator**

Paula Hickey **art editor** Sunday Telegraph Magazine

Suzanne Davies **senior designer** You Magazine

editorial

jason ford

2nd Floor
No 1 Tysoe Street
London
EC1R 4SA

t. 0171 278 8522

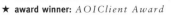

★ editorial section winner
★ award winner: *AOIClient Award*

title
Pop Opera
medium
Ink and acrylic
purpose of work
Illustrate magazine
article

brief
Popularisation of
opera
commissioned by
John Belknap /
Anne Braybon
company
The European

jason ford

2nd Floor
No 1 Tysoe Street
London
EC1R 4SA

t. 0171 278 8522

title
Hollywood Christmas
medium
Acrylic and ink
purpose of work
Illustration for classic Radio 2 drama programme

brief
In the radio remake of the 1954 film 'The Track of the Cat', a settler in the mountains of Nevada ignores the warnings of local Indians and sets out to track down a rogue cougar
commissioned by
Matthew Bookman
company
Radio Times
agent
Heart
t. 0171 833 4447

christopher corr

62
GB

27 Myddelton Street
London
EC1

t. 0171 833 5699

title
Christmas Livery
medium
Gouache on paper
purpose of work
To decorate the
five 'name' days
during Christmas

brief
Set of five
illustrations each
themed around the
days they appear
on, eg Christmas
Day, Boxing Day,
etc
commissioned by
Jonathan Christie
company
Radio Times

andy bridge

See Agent

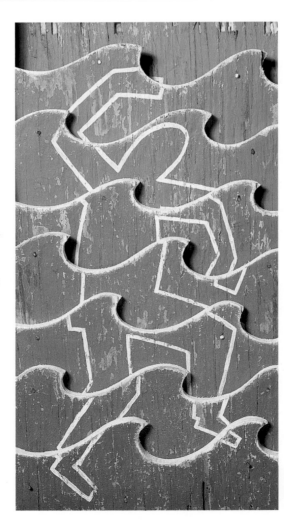

title
Deceit
medium
Mixed media
purpose of work
Illustration for
Radio 4 programme
brief
A former MP
disappears from his
yacht. His wife is
convinced he is
dead, but becomes
drawn into a web
of speculation and
gossip

commissioned by
Matthew Bookman
company
Radio Times
agent
The Inkshed
98 Columbia Road
London
E2
t. 0171 613 2323

148

debbie lush

Top Flat
10 Shipka Road
Balham
London
SW12 9QP

t. 0181 673 5100

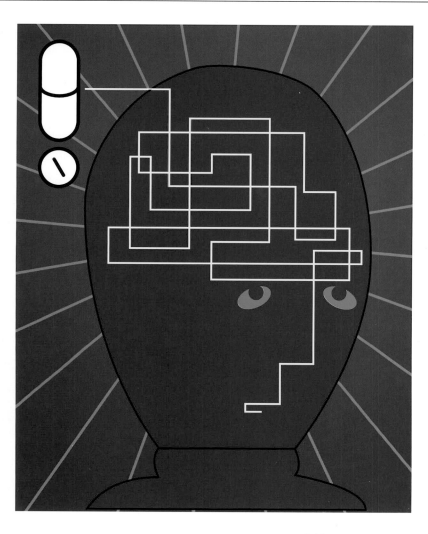

title
Fighting over
Beverley

medium
Acrylic

purpose of work
Illustration for
Radio 4 programme

brief
When Beverley
accompanies her
new American
husband home in
wartime, she left
behind a Yorkshire
man whom she had
promised to marry,
half a century on,
Archie decides to
win her back

commissioned by
Matthew Bookman

company
Radio Times

agent
The Inkshed
98 Columbia Road
London
E2 7QB
t. 0171 613 2323

kam tang

t. 0171 737 1113

title
Headaches From
Hell

medium
Computer
generated

purpose of work
Illustration for
Radio Times Health
Page

brief
Modern migraine
remedies can bring
relief - just ask
your GP

commissioned by
Nathan Gale

company
Radio Times

geoff grandfield

64
GB

30 Allen Road
London
N16 8SA

t. 0171 241 1523

title
Sweeney Todd
medium
Chalk pastel
purpose of work
Illustration for
Radio 3 concert
programme
brief
Sondheims grisly
musical tells of a
19th century street
barber who slits his
customer's throats
and turns their
bodies over to the
inventive Mrs
Lovett to bake into
pies

commissioned by
Matthew Bookman
company
Radio Times
agency
Heart
t. 0171 833 4447

---

sean lee

72 Promenade
Portobello
Edinburgh
EH15 2DX

t. 0131 657 4369

title
'Ready, Steady,
Cook!'
medium
Gouache
purpose of work
Illustration of
Ainsley Harriott

brief
Caricature of
exuberant, fast
talking chef,
Ainsley Harriott, for
his appearance on
BBC1's 'Ready,
Steady Cook!'
commissioned by
Mark Taylor
company
Radio Times

carolyn gowdy

2c Maynard Close
Off Cambia Street
London
SW6 2EN

t. 0171 731 5380

65

GB

title
The Trick is to keep
Breathing
medium
Mixed media
purpose of work
Illustration for
Radio 4 programme

brief
Bereavement
becomes the
catalyst for Joy's
emotional
breakdown in this
adaptation of
Janice Galloway's
award winning
novel
commissioned by
Matthew Bookman
company
Radio Times

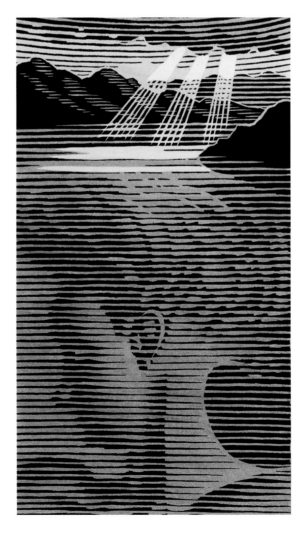

bill sanderson

Fernleigh
Huntington Road
Houghton
Cambridgeshire
PE17 2AV

t. 01480 461506

title
Board canvasses
medium
Scraper board and
inks
purpose of work
Illustration for
Radio 4 play

brief
The death of a
woman at a
reservoir scarcely
rates a mention in
the local press.
Although her father
is tipped off that
his daughter may
have been
murdered, the
police aren't
interested
commissioned by
Nathan Gale
company
Radio Times

kevin o'keefe

38 Osborne Road
Bristol
BS3 1PW

t. 0117 963 3835
f. 0117 963 3835

66
GB

title
Internet Addiction
medium
Ink and acrylic on acetate
purpose of work
Commissioned article for a computer magazine
brief
A small bedroom. It is night time. Someone is working happily on a computer. Atmosphere isolated but not negative or depressing
commissioned by
Susie Louis
company
VNU
agent
Black Hat
4 Northington Street
London WC1N 2JG
t. 0171 430 9146
f. 0171 430 9156

frank love

The Dairy
5-7 Marischal Road
London
SE13 5LE

t. 0181 297 2212
f. 0181 297 2212

title	commissioned by
Temps	Vera Naughton
medium	**company/client**
Mixed media	Wall Street Journal
purpose of work	**agent**
Illustrate article	Eastwing
brief	98 Columbia Road
Fitting the right	London
temporary staff	E2 7QB
	t. 0171 613 5580

68

GB

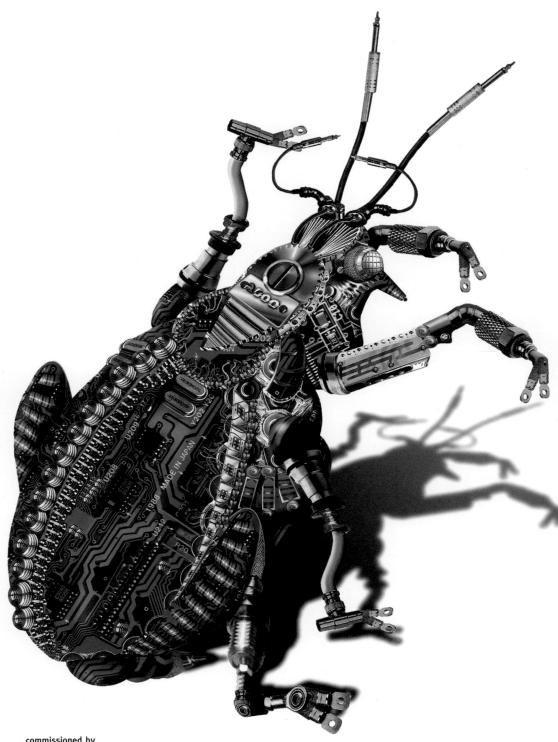

title
Millennium Bug

medium
Digital - Photoshop
and Live Picture

purpose of work
Article about the
possible computer
failure in year 2000

brief
To produce a
picture of the
millennium bug as
a kind of beetle
made of computer-
type hardware

commissioned by
Steve Lewis

company
The Publishing
Team Ltd

client
BUPA

agent
Illustration
1 Vicarage Crescent
Clapham
London SW11 3LP
t. 0171 228 8882

max ellis

See Agent

title	commissioned by
Channel Crossing	Paul Kurjeja
medium	**company/client**
Digital montage	Dennis Publishing
purpose of work	**agent**
Magazine feature	Illustration
brief	1 Vicarage Crescent
Mackintosh are	Clapham
producing software	London SW11 3LP
to allow pc	t. 0171 228 8882
programs to be	
run. Illustrate this	
dangerous new	
environment being	
entered into	

stuart briers

186 Ribblesdale
Road
London
SW16 6QY

t. 0181 677 6203
f. 0181 677 6203

★ **winner:** *Daler and Rowney*
- best use of traditional materials

DALER~ROWNEY
TRUSTED by ARTISTS WORLDWIDE

70
GB

title
Care to fit the bill
medium
Acrylic
purpose of work
Editorial illustration
brief
To accompany
article about care
for the sufferers of
MS which typically
attacks the spinal
cord
commissioned by
Nancy Yuill
company/client
Health Which

title
Judge Not?
medium
Acrylic
purpose of work
Editorial illustration
brief
To accompany an
article which takes
a very critical look
at those who award
literary prizes

commissioned by
Susan Buchanen
company
Buchanen Davey
client
Prospect Magazine

MAGNET
ARTISTS

andrew bylo

Clockwork Studios
38b Southwell Road
London
SE5 9PG

t. 0171 274 4116
f. 0171 738 3743
www.aoi.co.uk/bylo

71

GB

title
Macaws
medium
Watercolour and
gouache
purpose of work
Self promotional
brief
Painted from life in
private aviary

MAGNET
ARTISTS

ali pellatt

63 Nevis Road
London
SW17 7QL

t. 0181 772 0332
f. 0181 772 0332
mobile. 0402 748619

72
GB

title
Scooby Snacks

medium
Montage,
neopastels and
spray paint

purpose of work
Jacket: Times
Directory

brief
A humorous
portrait of generic
pop star and his
food on tour

commissioned by
David Driver

company
The Times

MAGNET
ARTISTS

anna steinberg

57A Linden Avenue
Kensal Rise
London
NW10 5RG

t. 0181 964 1069
f. 0181 964 1069
pager. 01426 355 030

title
Eating out

medium
Ink and Pastel

purpose of work
in-flight magazine
article

brief
Business lunches
are the health bane
of the modern
executive

commissioned by
Mike Wescombe

company/client
International High
Flyer

MAGNET
ARTISTS

alan alder

Flat 6
41 Craven Hill Gardens
London
W2 3EA

t. 0171 240 8925 (UK)
t. 0046 21 41 22 00 (Sweden)

74
GB

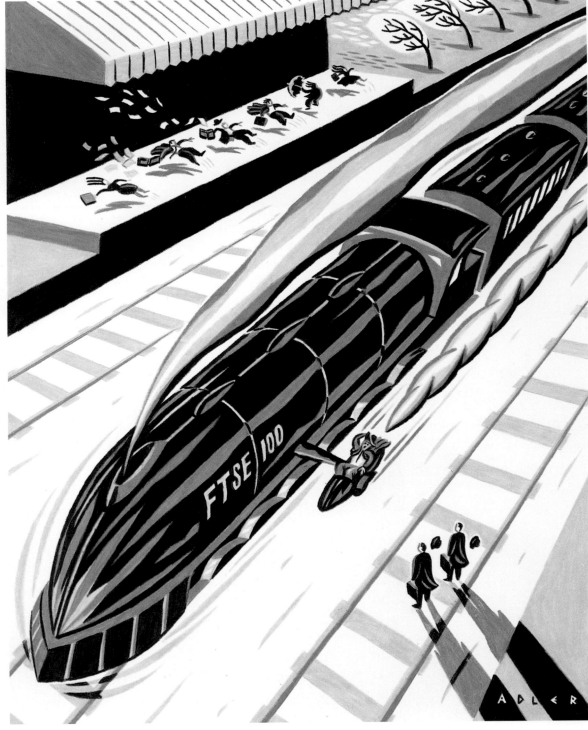

title
Tracker Fund

medium
Pencil

purpose of work
To illustrate
Newspaper article

brief
To show how
personal tracker
funds perform at
the same rate as
the 100 top
performing UK
shares : the FTSE
100

commissioned by
David Driver

company
News International

client
The Times

agent
CIA
36 Wellington
Street
London WC2
t. 0171 240 8925

veronica bailey

188 Langham Road
Turnpike Lane
London
N15 3NB

t. 0181 888 0606
f. 0181 374 1891

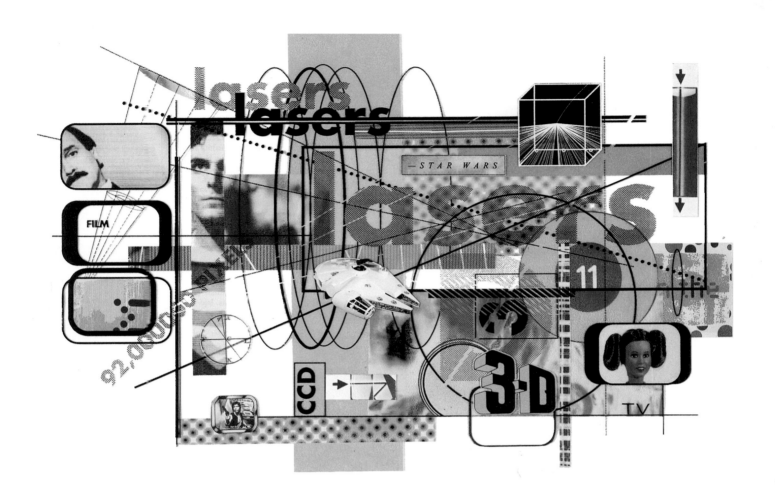

title
Holographic TV
medium
Collage and
computer
generated
purpose of work
Editorial spread for
New Scientist

brief
Illustrate how
holograms work
with reference to
its use in film
commissioned by
Deborah George
company/client
New Scientist
agent
Debut Art
30 Tottenham
Street
London
W1 9PN
t. 0171 636 1064

zafer & barbara baran

47 Kings Road
Richmond
Surrey
TW10 6EG

t. 0181 948 3050
f. 0181 948 3050

title
Volunteer

medium
Liquid watercolour
and ink

purpose of work
Magazine
illustration

brief
To illustrate article
'Redefining the
voluntary sector',
published in the
Royal Society of
Arts Journal

commissioned by
Mike Dempsey

company
CDT Design

client
Royal Society of
Arts

zafer & barbara baran

47 Kings Road
Richmond
Surrey
TW10 6EG

t. 0181 948 3050
f. 0181 948 3050

title
Egg Heads

medium
Liquid watercolour
and ink

purpose of work
Illustration for
newspaper
supplement

brief
To illustrate article
on the Disability
Discrimination Act

commissioned by
Mary Jane Bogue

company/client
Daily Telegraph

title
Hi-tech Toilet

medium
Liquid watercolour
and ink

purpose of work
Illustration for
newspaper
supplement

brief
To illustrate article
'Japanese offer the
world hi-tech toilet
training'

commissioned by
David Riley

company/client
Daily Telegraph

bill butcher

Sans Works
1 Sans Walk
London
EC1R 5oLT

t. 0171 336 6642
f. 0171 251 2642

78
GB

title
Playing with Fire
medium
Acrylic
purpose of work
Lloyds list front
cover
brief
To illustrate the
RISK of natural
disasters focusing
on the dangers of
forest fires
commissioned by
Nick Blaxall
company
Lloyds List

title
Jet Jam
medium
Collage acrylic
purpose of work
Editorial piece for
European
brief
To illustrate build
up of air traffic at
European airports
commissioned by
John Belknap
company
The European

linda combi

17 Albemarle Road
York
YO23 1EW

t. 01904 623036
f. 01904 623036

PRIVATE FUNCTION

title
Private Dining
Room
medium
Inks
purpose of work
Illustration for
article on private
dining rooms

brief
To humorously
depict the idea of
private dining
rooms in
restaurants where
discretion would be
assured
commissioned by
Tracey Young
company/client
Tatler Magazine

jill calder

20 Henderson Street
Flat 3F2
Leith
Edinburgh
EH6 6BS

t. 0131 553 2986
f. 0131 553 2986
email: Jill.C@btinternet.com

80
GB

title
Mr Director

medium
Ink collage

purpose of work
Illustrates Honor
Fraser's weekly
column for
Scotland on
Sunday Newspaper

brief
Open brief

commissioned by
Sandra Colamartino

company
Scotsman
Publications Ltd

client
Spectrum Magazine

jill calder

20 Henderson Street
Flat 3F2
Leith
Edinburgh
EH6 6BS

t. 0131 553 2986
f. 0131 553 2986
email: Jill.C@btinternet.com

81

GB

title
Sitting Room
Habits
medium
Ink
purpose of work
Illustrates Honor
Fraser's weekly
column for
Scotland on
Sunday Newspaper

brief
Open brief
commissioned by
Sandra Colamartino
company
Scotsman
Publications Ltd
client
Spectrum Magazine

title
Fitba' Daft
medium
Ink
purpose of work
Illustrates Honor
Fraser's weekly
column for
Scotland on
Sunday Newspaper

brief
Open brief
commissioned by
Sandra Colamartino
company
Scotsman
Publications Ltd
client
Spectrum Magazine

title
Le Driver
medium
Ink collage
purpose of work
Illustrates Honor
Fraser's weekly
column for
Scotland on
Sunday Newspaper

brief
Open brief
commissioned by
Sandra Colamartino
company
Scotsman
Publications Ltd
client
Spectrum Magazine

cyrus deboo

57 Ormonde Court
Upper Richmond Road
London
SW15 6TP

t. 0181 788 8167
f. 0181 788 8167
mobile. 07050 039 477

82
GB

title
Room with a view

medium
Computer
generated -
Illustrator 7

purpose of work
Editorial

brief
To create an
abstract and non
obvious illustration
for a review about
two CD systems
(games and
movies) for home
entertainment

commissioned by
Alex Westthorpe

company
Computer Shopper

title
High Flyer

medium
Computer
generated -
Illustrator 7

purpose of work
Editorial

brief
To create an
illustration about
flight and fatigue.
To get plenty of
sleep - a glass of
wine will help

commissioned by
Gary Lockerby

company
YOU Magazine

philip disley

34 East Wapping
Quay
Liverpool
L3 4BU

t. 0151 709 9126

title	brief
The New Culture Club	To illustrate an article on the new
medium	art establishment
Ink	**commissioned by**
purpose of work	Kate Dwyer
Editorial illustration	**company**
	Frank

jovan djordjevic

9 Fairlop Road
Leytonstone
London
E11 1BL

t. 0181 539 3892
f. 0181 539 3893
e-mail. jovan@jovan.demon.co.uk

84
GB

title
Why Training Fails

medium
Montage, ink,
photocopy, digital
output

purpose of work
To illustrate
remedial actions
within management

brief
Open interpretation

commissioned by
Peter Drake

company
VNU Business
Publications
Management
Consultancy

jovan djordjevic

9 Fairlop Road
Leytonstone
London
E11 1BL

t. 0181 539 3892
f. 0181 539 3893
e-mail. jovan@jovan.cmon.co.uk

85
GB

title
Cannabis Crossfire
medium
Montage,
watercolour,
photocopy, digital
output
purpose of work
Positive/negative -
professional/legal
debate over
medical use of
cannabis

brief
Open interpretation
commissioned by
Ned Campbell
company
Wolff Olins Ltd
client
Vision Magazine

jasper goodall

25c Jeffreys Road
Clapham
London
SW4 6QU

t. 0958 306 988
website: www.sonnet.co.uk/madforit/jasper
email: jasper_goodall@hotmail.com

title
Dudley Smith

medium
Digital

purpose of work
To illustrate a
literary character

brief
Visual portrayal of
fictional character
to introduce people
to writers they may
not have heard of

commissioned by
Ash Gibson

company
GQ Magazine

title
Skink

medium
Digital

purpose of work
To illustrate a
literary character

brief
Visual portrayal of
fictional character
to introduce people
to writers they may
not have heard of

commissioned by
Ash Gibson

company
GQ Magazine

adam graff

10 St Columbas
House
16 Prospect Hill
Walthamstow
London
E17 3EZ

t. 0181 521 7182
f. 0181 521 7182

title		**commissioned by**
Tobacco Emporia		Time Out
medium		**client**
Chinagraph and		Time Out Magazine
computer		Ltd
purpose of work		**agent**
Editorial		The Organisation
brief		69 Caledonian
To head an article		Road
on London's		London
specialist tobacco		N1 9BT
emporia		t. 0171 833 8268

nick hardcastle

14 Loxley Road
London
SW18 3LJ

t. 0181 871 1748
f. 0181 871 1748

88
GB

title
Bumper harvest
medium
Pen and ink with
watercolour
purpose of work
Illustration for
Brain Waves
column in Weekend
Guardian

brief
To illustrate the
phrase "bumper
Harvest" in a
humorous fashion
commissioned by
Chris Maslanka
company/client
Weekend Guardian
agent
Illustrators.Co
3 Richborne
Terrace
London
SW8 1AR
t. 0171 793 7000

jo hassall

Represented by
Private View

t. 0181 299 1392

89

GB

title	**brief**
Green Trees	To illustrate
medium	ecologically sound
Mixed media	business practice
	leading to growth
purpose of work	
For Prudential	**commissioned by**
in-house magazine	Harry McFarland
	company
	Perception Design
	client
	Prudential

<footer>
175
·

EDITORIAL
</footer>

kevin hauff

7 Pendre Avenue
Prestatyn
Denbighshire
LL19 9SH

t. 01745 888734
f. 01745 888734

90

GB

title
The Alchemist

medium
Acrylic/collage

purpose of work
Economist special
supplement cover

brief
To illustrate an
economist
supplement cover
entitled The
Alchemist,
depicting a
medieval
Alchemist's shock
at the new
methods of drug
design and
development

commissioned by
Una Corrigan

company
The Economist

frazer hudson

150 Curtain Road
1st Floor Studio,
Back Building
London
EC2A 3AR

t. 0973 616 054
f. 0171 613 4434

title
Barking Mad

medium
Mixed media

purpose of work
Science illustration

brief
To illustrate the science behind quarantine highlighting the new passport rules this brings about

commissioned by
Naomi Depeza

company
The Independent on Sunday Review

satoshi kambayashi

Flat 2
40 Tisbury Road
Hove
East Sussex
BN3 3BA

t. 01273 771539
f. 01273 771539

title
Decline of British
Literature

medium
India Ink and
watercolour

purpose of work
An editorial spot
illustration

brief
To illustrate an
essay about the
decline of quality
literature in Britain

commissioned by
Susan Buchanan

company
Buchanan-Davey

client
Prospect

agent
Ian Fleming
72-74 Brewer
Street
London
WIR 3PH
t. 0171 734 8701

satoshi kambayashi

Flat 2
40 Tisbury Road
Hove
East Sussex
BN3 3BA

t. 01273 771539
f. 01273 771535

title
Please Give

medium
Ink and
watercolour

purpose of work
An editorial spot
illustration

brief
For an article about
the ever-decreasing
amount of tipping
in hotels

commissioned by
Adrian Hulf

company
Illustrated London
News Group

client
*First Class
Magazine*

agent
Ian Fleming
72-74 Brewer
Street
London
W1R 3PH
t. 0171 734 8701

peter knock

17 Nelson Drive
Leigh on Sea
Essex
SS9 1DA

t. 01702 476885
f. 01702 476885

94

GB

title
Elvis Costello and
John Harle
medium
Watercolour
purpose of work
Magazine
Illustration

brief
Double portrait of
two musicians for a
review of their
collaborated
material
commissioned by
Robert Priest
company
Esquire Magazine
(US)
client
American Esquire

henning löhlein

Bristol Craft &
Design Centre
6 Leonard Lane
Bristol
BS1 1EA

t. 0117 9299077
f. 0117 9299077

title
Christmas Quiz

medium
Acrylic

purpose of work
Cover Illustration
for the Saturday
Times magazine

brief
To find a striking
image for the
Christmas quiz
cover

commissioned by
D Curless

company
The Times

anne magill

See Agent

t. 0468 362420

title
Missing You

medium
Acrylic on paper

purpose of work
To illustrate a
fiction piece

brief
To depict the figure
of the woman
central to the story
as she ponders her
failed marriage

commissioned by
Lorraine Older

company
South Bank
Publishing Group

client
Woman and Home
Magazine

agent
The Inkshed
98 Columbia Road
London
E2 7QB
t. 0171 613 2323

james marsh

21 Elms Road
London
SW4 9ER

t. 0171 622 9530
f. 0171 498 6851

97
GB

title
Madonna's Child
medium
Acrylic on canvas
purpose of work
To illustrate
fictional story in
magazine

brief
Open brief to
illustrate story
about a girl who
thinks she is the
madonna's child
commissioned by
Susan Buchanan
company
Buchanan Davey
client
Prospect Magazine

glen mcbeth

12, 37 Sandport
Street
Edinburgh
EH6 6EP

t. 0131 555 0576
f. 0131 555 0576

Mr Bun the Baker
Mr Bun the Baker

Mr Bun Jnr
Mr Bun Jnr

Mrs Bun the Baker's wife
Mrs Bun the Baker's wife

Brother Bun
Brother Bun

Miss Bun Jnr
Miss Bun Jnr

Mrs Bun Jnr
Mrs Bun Jnr

Ex- Mrs Bun Jnr
Ex- Mrs Bun Jnr

Grandson Bun
Grandson Bun

Grandson Bun
Grandson Bun

Granddaughter Bun
Granddaughter Bun

Cousin Bun
Cousin Bun

Grandson Bun
Grandson Bun

Uncle Bun
Uncle Bun

Cousin Bun
Cousin Bun

Baby Bun
Baby Bun

Aunty Bun
Aunty Bun

Distant Cousin Bun
Distant Cousin Bun

Great Cousin Bun
Great Cousin Bun

Long Lost Brother Bun
Long Lost Brother Bun

Second Cousin Twice Removed Bun
Second Cousin Twice Removed Bun

title
The Buns
medium
Pen ink collage
colour copy
purpose of work
Magazine
illustrations

brief
To produce happy
family cards to
show how
everyone from
close family to
distant relatives
want a part of a
family business
commissioned by
Jane Greig
company
CA Magazine

shane mcgowan

23A Parkholme
Road
London
E8 3AG

t. 0171 249 6444
f. 0171 249 6444

title
First person
feminine

medium
Gouache, ink

purpose of work
To illustrate article
in the 'Real Life'
section

brief
To show how men
narrate novels
through female
heroines

commissioned by
Mark Hayman

company/client
*The Independent
on Sunday*

agent
The Organisation
69 Caledonian
Road
London N1
t. 0171 833 8268

tony mcsweeney

4 Water Lane
Richmond
Surrey
TW9 1TJ

t. 0181 940 2425
f. 0181 940 2425

100
GB

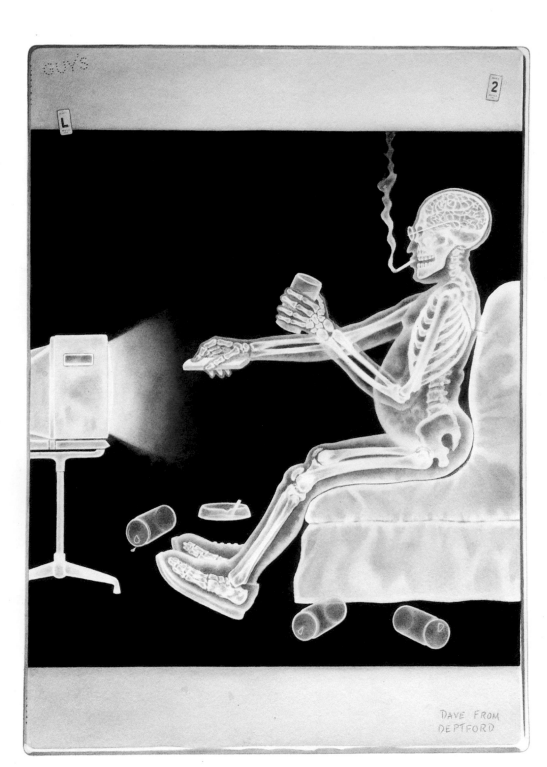

title
Power to the
People
medium
Watercolour
gouache
purpose of work
To illustrate an
article in ES
magazine

brief
To provide a
convincing looking
x-ray of a couch
potato watching TV
during World Cup
'98
commissioned by
Robin Hedges
company
Associated
Newspapers
client
*Evening Standard
Magazine*

kate newington

30 Saltoun Road
London
SW2 1EP

t. 0171 274 1418
f. 0171 274 1418

title
Anthony Powell
medium
Mixed media on
paper
purpose of work
Commission for the
Observer
Newspaper

brief
An illustration for a
profile of the writer
Anthony Powell
whose series of
novels 'A Dance to
the Music of Time'
had just been
dramatised for TV
commissioned by
The Observer

chris robson

13 Whatley Road
Clifton, Bristol
BS8 2PS

t. 01179 737694
f. 01179 737694
mobile. 0797 137 9354
e-mail. cbrobson@aol.com

102
GB

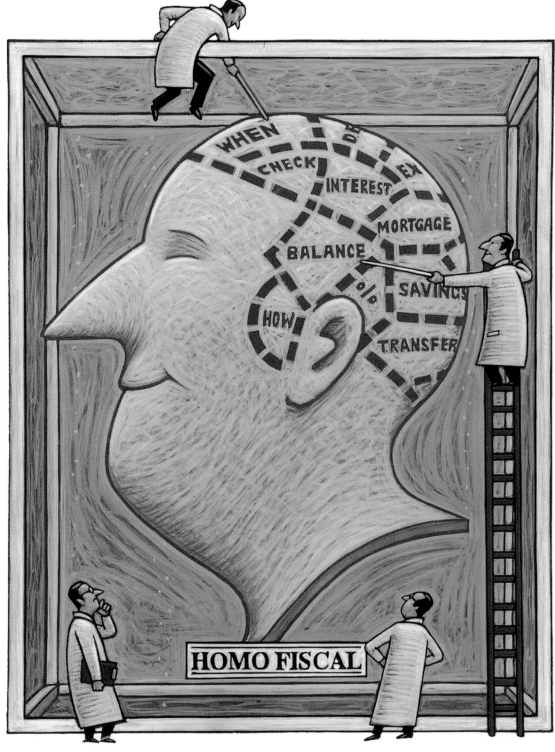

title
Homo Fiscal

medium
Acrylic

purpose of work
Magazine
Illustration

brief
To show how
financiers make
decisions

commissioned by
Jane Ure-Smith

company
TPD Publishing

client
Talking Business
Magazine

andrew selby

9 Perryfield
Matching Green
Essex
CM17 0PY

t. 01279 731452 /
0973 271449
f. 01279 731452

title
All Change

medium
Watercolour

purpose of work
Editorial

brief
Changing your
company name can
make you more
appealing to a
wider audience

commissioned by
Karen Falconer

company
Dennis Publishing

penny sobr

Omnibus Centre
Unit 35
39-41 North Road
London
N7 9DP

t. 0171 609 3979
f. 0171 607 4652

104
GB

title
Ascot Fashion

medium
Gouache

purpose of work
Illustrate
Newspaper article

brief
What to wear this
year at Ascot

commissioned by
John Belknap /
Julian Bovis

company
Sunday Business

peter till

11 Berkeley Road
London
N8 8RU

t. 0181 341 0497
f. 0181 341 0497

title
Triangle
medium
Pen, ink and
watercolour
purpose of work
For magazine
article
brief
Article about
science being
based on first
principles
commissioned by
Colin Brewster
company
New Scientist

title
Chip Art
medium
Pen, ink and
watercolour
purpose of work
To accompany
article
brief
Given a brief news
item about
computers - here
computer art
commissioned by
Peter Kirwan
company
VNU
client
Computing

judges

Carolyn Gowdy **illustrator**
Peter Cotton **art director** Little Brown Books
Ami Smithson **senior designer** Penguin Books
Bob Hollingsworth **senior designer** Random House
Nick Castle **art director** Orion Publishing

nelly dimitranova

Top Flat
33 Savernake Road
London
NW3 2JU

t. 0171 284 2334

title
Heroes Like Us
medium
Acrylic and crayon
purpose of work
Book Jacket
brief
The book
commissioned by
Harvill Press
client
Christopher
Maclehose

geoff grandfield

30 Allen Road
London
N16 8SA

t. 0171 241 1523
f. 0171 241 1523
e-mail. g.grandfield@mdx.ac.uk

title
Brighton Rock

medium
Chalk pastel

purpose of work
Book Illustration

brief
Read the novel

commissioned by
Joe Whitlock-
Blundell

company/client
The Folio Society

title
A Burnt Out Case

medium
Chalk pastel

purpose of work
Book Illustration

brief
Read the novel

commissioned by
Joe Whitlock-
Blundell

company/client
The Folio Society

geoff grandfield

30 Allen Road
London
N16 8SA

t. 0171 241 1523
f. 0171 241 1523
e-mail. g.grandfield@mdx.ac.uk

GB

title
The Power and the
Glory
medium
Chalk pastel
purpose of work
Book Illustration
brief
Read the novel
commissioned by
Joe Whitlock-
Blundell
company/client
The Folio Society

title
The End of the
Affair
medium
Chalk pastel
purpose of work
Book Illustration
brief
Read the novel
commissioned by
Joe Whitlock-
Blundell
company/client
The Folio Society

lesley hilling

152 Mayall Road
London
SW24 oPH

t. 0171 737 2689
f. 0171 733 1845
e-mail. offbeat@dircon.co.uk

title
The Search

medium
Digital image

purpose of work
Book jacket

brief
To illustrate one man's search for a group of 89 boys who all survived Birkenau concentration camp

commissioned by
Serpent's Tail

company
Serpent's Tail Books

client
Peter Ayrton

harry horse

20 Bruntsfield
Gardens
Edinburgh
EH10 4EA

t. 0131 228 4196
f. 0131 228 4196

title
Fup

medium
Mixed media,
shelac and ink

purpose of work
Illustrate novel

brief
To illustrate Jim
Dodge's novel
about two hillbillies
and one duck
called Fup

commissioned by
Jamie Byng

company/client
Canongate Books

agency
Caroline Sheldon
Literary Agency
London Farm
Whiteoaks Lane
Shalfleet
PO30 4NU
t. 01983 531826

peter simon jones

72 Forthill Road
Broughty Ferry
Dundee
Scotland
DD5 3DN

t. 01382 738444
e-mail. p.s.jones@dundee.ac.uk

114
GB

title
Sai Kung, Hong Kong

medium
Monoprint

purpose of work
Illustration for a book entitled Hong Kong Visual diary

brief
Double Page Spread illustrating a way of life in changing Hong Kong

commissioned by
Mandarin Publishers

title
Tai Long Village

medium
Acrylic/watercolour on canvas board

purpose of work
One of a series of illustrations depicting various aspects of Hong Kong life and culture

brief
Double Page illustration from the book 'Hong Kong A Diary', depicting rural life in the New Territories, Hong Kong

commissioned by
Mandarin Publishers

anne magill

See Agent

t. 0468 362420

title
Julia Alone

medium
Acrylic on paper

purpose of work
Book jacket - Julia Alone by Ann Stevens

brief
To portray Julia, sitting alone, the Thames and Putney Bridge to be behind her. The portrait was not to be too specific but had to hint at her sadness and loneliness

commissioned by
Sonia Dobie

company/client
Harper Collins

agent
The Inkshed
98 Columbia Road
London
E2 7QB
t. 0171 613 2323

james marsh

21 Elms Road
London
SW4 9ER

t. 0171 622 9530
f. 0171 498 6851

116
GB

title
A cat's Tail

medium
Acrylic on canvas

purpose of work
Page in Best Ever
Book of Cats

brief
To illustrate Thai
legend: Why the
Siamese cat has a
kink in its tail

commissioned by
Sue Aldworth

company
Kingfisher Books

client
Larousse plc

daren mason

Echo Beach Studio
19 Muspole Street
Norwich
NR3 1DJ

t. 01603 630 500
mobile. 0410 769203
f. 01603 630 500
e.mail. daren.mason@btinternet.com

117

GB

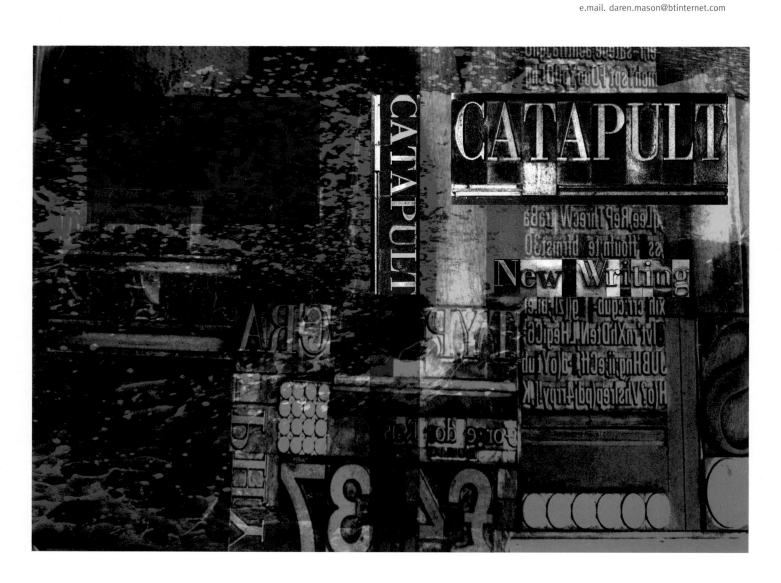

title
Catapult

medium
Photography and
computer

purpose of work
Book jacket

brief
Book jacket for MA
Creative Writing
course UEA

commissioned by
UEA/CCPA
Centre for Creative
& Performing Arts

sarah perkins

37e Guinness Court
Snowfields
London
SE1 3SX

t. 0171 378 1510
f. 0171 357 6442

title
Orchard on Fire
medium
Mixed
purpose of work
Book jacket
brief
Read the book
commissioned by
Ami Smithson
company
Reed Consumer
Books
agent
The Inkshed
98 Columbia Road
London E2 7QB

title
A Running Tide
medium
Mixed
purpose of work
Book jacket
brief
Illustrate the book
telling the story of
a girls childhood
memories in Maine,
America
commissioned by
Juliet Rowley
company
Random House
agent
The Inkshed
98 Columbia Road
London E2 7QB

sarah perkins

37e Guinness Court
Snowfields
London
SE1 3SX

t. 0171 378 1510
f. 0171 357 6442

title
A Way of Being
Free - Ben Okri

medium
Mixed

purpose of work
Book jacket

brief
The idea of words
liberating the
person,
transporting a mind
to another place,
freedom

commissioned by
Nick Castle

company
Orion

agent
The Inkshed
98 Columbia Road
London E2 7QB

ian pollock

171 Bond Street
Macclesfield
Cheshire
SK11 6RE

t. 01625 426205
f. 01625 261390

'120
GB

title
The Corporate Fool
medium
Watercolour ink
and gouache
purpose of work
Book jacket

brief
Book jacket for The
Corporate Fool by
David Firth
commissioned by
Capstone
Publishing Limited
agent
The Inkshed
98 Columbia Road
London
E2 7QB
t. 0171 613 2323

nancy tolford

The Coach House
23 Rushmore Road
Clapton
London
E5 0ET

t. 0181 985 8377
f. 0181 985 8377

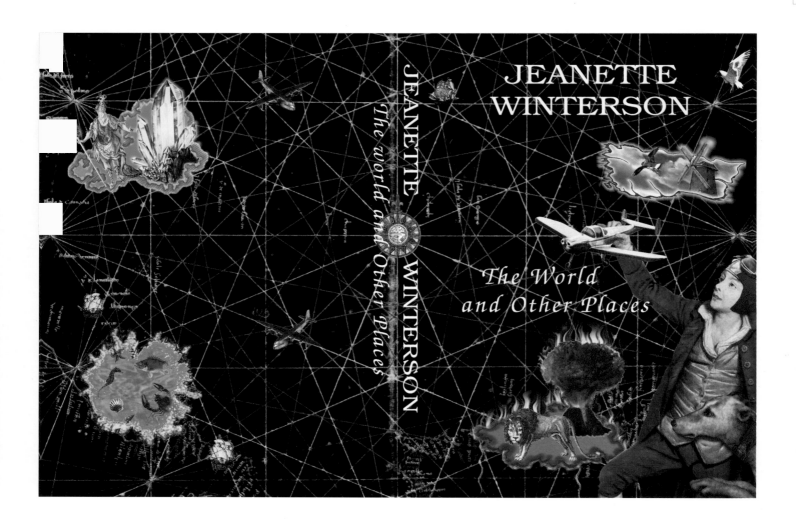

title
The World and
Other Places

medium
Computer
generated

purpose of work
Book jacket

brief
Collection of short
stories, involving
travel to both real
and imaginary
places. By
Jeannette
Winterson

commissioned by
Caz Hildebrand

company
Random House UK

borin van loon

117 Belle Vue Road
Ipswich
Suffolk
IP4 2RD

t. 01473 421529
e-mail. borin@vanloon.keme.co.uk

title
"Oh goodie, it's
the po-mo bit
next!"

medium
Brush and ink with
'paper-print' on
paper

purpose of work
Book illustration

brief
To provide a full-
page facial image
with a post-
modernist twist.

title
Ashis Nandy

medium
Ink, brush and
fingerprint on
paper

purpose of work
Book illustration

brief
Portrait of Nandy,
psychologist and
cultural critic.

Oh goodie,
it's the po-mo
bit next!

all images from
"Cultural Studies
for Beginners"

commissioned by
Richard
Appignanesi

company/client
Icon Books Ltd

title
Antonio Gramsci

medium
Dip pen on paper

purpose of work
Book illustration

brief
To illustrate the
Marxist thinker
Gramsci who
devised the term
"Subaltern"
studies.

rosemary woods

2 Gosberton Road
London
SW12 8LF

t. + 44 (0) 207 378 1219
f. + 44 (0) 208 673 6700

title
Buhari Steam

medium
Acrylic on paper

purpose of work
Little Indian Cook
Book

brief
To give a flavour of
India and include
some of the
ingredients of
Buhari Gosht

commissioned by
John Murphy

company/client
Appletree Press

title
Coconut Coast

medium
Acrylic on paper

purpose of work
Little Indian Cook
Book

brief
To give a flavour of
India for chilli
coconut sauce
recipe

commissioned by
John Murphy

company/client
Appletree Press

judges

Roger Walton **art director** Duncan Baird

Nick Clark **art director** Readers Digest General Books

Les Hayes **creative executive** London Transport Advertising and Publicity

Colin Wilkin **illustrator**

Bill O'Neill **editor** Guardian On Line

information

angela harland

Haven Cottage
Atlow
Ashbourne
Derbyshire
DE6 1NS

t. 01335 370992

★ information section winner

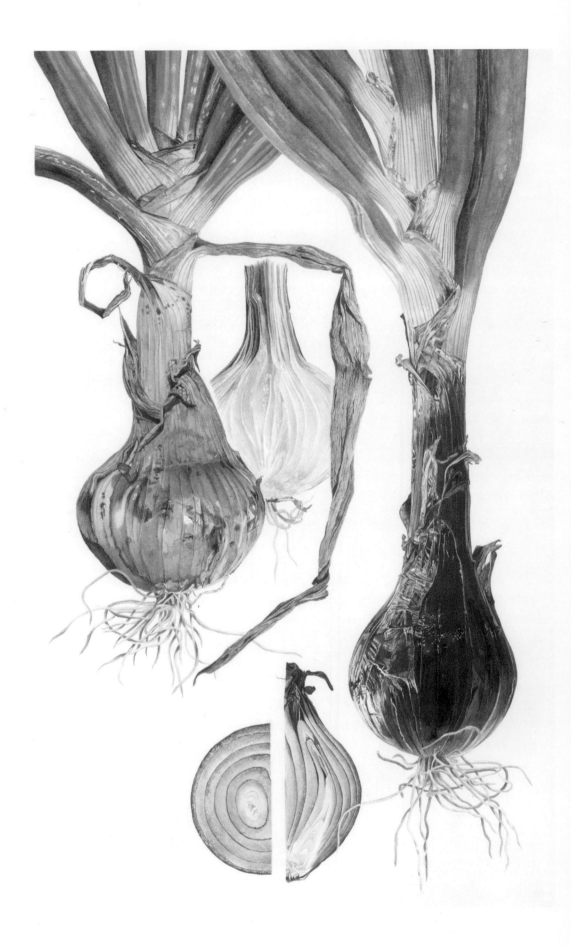

title
Onions

medium
Watercolour

purpose of work
Degree illustration
project work

brief
Botanical

submitted by
Blackpool and The
Fylde College

paul bimrose

43 Lee Moor Road
Stanley
Wakefield
WF3 4EF

t. 01924 826625

title
Pheasant
Dissection

medium
Watercolour
Gouache

purpose of work
Degree illustration

brief
Professional media
brief, Year 3

submitted by
Blackpool and The
Fylde College

title
Shed

medium
Watercolour
Gouache

purpose of work
Degree illustration
project work

brief
Professional media
brief, Year 3

submitted by
Blackpool and The
Fylde College

mark holmes

7 Holly Dene
Armthorpe
Doncaster
South Yorkshire
DN3 2HJ

t. 01302 834066

title
Still Life with Jack
Daniels and jacket

medium
Acrylic

purpose of work
Degree project
work

brief
Professional media
brief

submitted by
Blackpool and The
Fylde College

christopher jacks

35 Keswick Drive
Frodsham
Cheshire
WA6 7LT

t. 01928 732067
mobile.
07957 330322

jeremy glover

13 North Drive
High Legh
Knutsford
Cheshire
WA16 6LX

t. 01925 754834

129
GB

title
Focke Wulf 190A8
medium
Conventional pencil
stage: rendered in
Adobe Illustrator
purpose of work
Degree project
work

brief
Team project year
two evolution of
technology
submitted by
Blackpool and The
Fylde College

anne louise jennings

Domus,
Woodland Avenue
Scarisbrick
Ormskirk
Lancs
L40 9QL

t. 01704 880654
f. 01704 880654

130

GB

title
Still life with
cheese board

medium
Watercolour

purpose of work
Degree project
work

brief
Professional media
brief

submitted by
Blackpool and The
Fylde College

elaine kenyon

West End Farm
Ingleton
Darlington
County Durham
DL2 3HS

t. 01325 730335

title
Cowslip
medium
Watercolour and
gouache
purpose of work
BA (Hons) Degree
project work
brief
Botanical - exam
project
submitted by
Blackpool and The
Fylde College

jonathan latimer

92 Swinley Road
Wigan
Lancs
WN1 2DL

t. 01942 230502

title
Biscuits

medium
Acrylic

purpose of work
Degree project
work

brief
Year three
professional media
brief

title
Strandline

medium
Acrylic

purpose of work
Degree project
work

brief
Year three final
project; Strandline
ecosystem

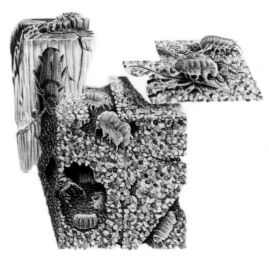

218

alastair miller

11 Priory Close
Deeping St. James
Peterborough
Lincs
PE6 8PR

t. 01778 342787

133
GB

title
Cycle Hub

medium
Form Z Auto Des
Sys

purpose of work
Degree project
work

brief
Cut away
promotional
illustration
Winner of "The
Form Z Award of
Distinction 1998" in
the category for
visualisation and
illustration

submitted by
Blackpool and The
Fylde College

stephen palmer

227 Ainsworth
Road
Radcliffe
Manchester
M26 4EE

134
GB

title
AJS Motorcycle

medium
Conventional pencil
stage through to
full digital

purpose of work
Degree Project
work

brief
Main illustration for
motorcycle
museum

submitted by
Blackpool and The
Fylde College

stuart rowbottom

The Grange
Haycroft Lane
Fleet
Nr. Holbeach
Spalding
Lincs
PE12 8LB

t. 01406 424005

135

GB

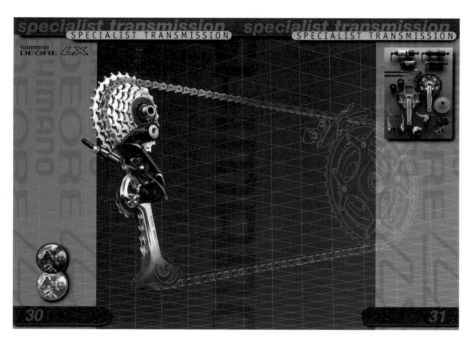

title
Shimano Gear
System

medium
Digital: Illustrator
and Photoshop

purpose of work
Degree project
work

brief
Form and function
brief: editorial/
promotional
information
illustration poster

submitted by
Blackpool and The
Fylde College

title
Architectural visual

medium
Auto Des Sys Form
Z Renderzone

purpose of work
Degree project
work

brief
Visualization of
proposed building
evolution of
technology brief

submitted by
Blackpool and The
Fylde College

title
Architectural visual

medium
Auto Des Sys Form
Z Renderzone

purpose of work
Degree project
work

brief
Visualization of
proposed building
evolution of
technology brief

submitted by
Blackpool and The
Fylde College

221

INFORMATION

william smith

24 Merton Road
Daventry
Northants
NN11 4RR

t. 01327 705331

136
GB

INFORMATION

title
Wasp's Nest
medium
Acrylic
purpose of work
Degree project
work
brief
Final project
submitted by
Blackpool and The
Fylde College

brian turner

63 Honeybourne
Belgrave
Tamworth
Staffs
B77 2JG

title
Power Transfer
Gearbox

medium
Auto Des Form Z
Render
Zone/Photoshop

purpose of work
Degree project
work

brief
Promotional
information poster

submitted by
Blackpool and The
Fylde College

martin wilcock

213 Brownhill Drive
Blackburn
Lancashire
BB1 9SB

t. 01254 245742

138
GB

title
Hay Meadow

medium
Watercolour

purpose of work
Degree project
work

brief
Live project -
Northern Hay
Meadows

submitted by
Blackpool and The
Fylde College

andrew wood

78 Warwick Road
Alkrington
Middleton
Manchester
M24 1HX

t. 0161 653 3955

title
Skeleton

medium
Acrylic

purpose of work
Degree project
work

brief
Evolution

submitted by
Blackpool and The
Fylde College

jean hawke

16 St Michael's
Close
Aylsham
Norwich
Norfolk
NR11 6HA

t. 01263 732693
f. 01263 732693

140
GB

title
Worstead Station
medium
Pen and ink and
watercolour wash
purpose of work
Illustration
brief
To show the quality
of the building in
its environment

title
Buckinghamshire
Arms, Blickling
medium
Pen and ink and
watercolour wash
purpose of work
Illustration
brief
To show the quality
of the building in
its environment

title
Blickling Orangery
medium
Pen and ink and
watercolour wash
purpose of work
Illustration
brief
To show the quality
of the building in
its environment

annabel milne

Grooms Cottage
Elsenham hall
Hertfordshire
CM22 6DP

t. 01279 814923
f. 01279 814962

GB

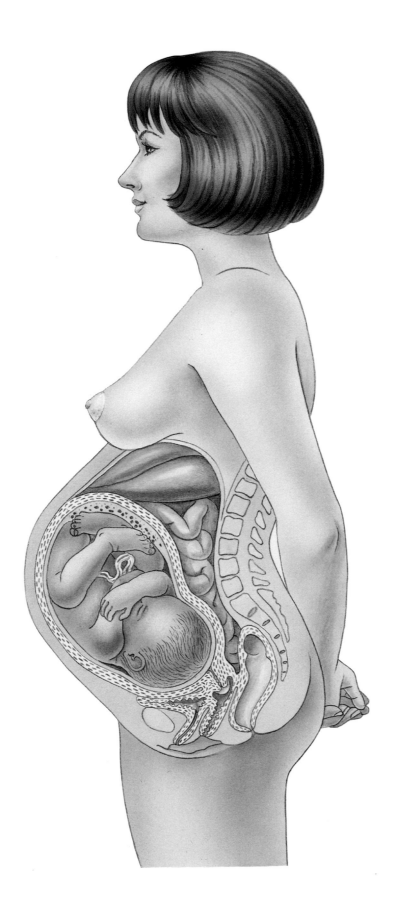

title
31 - 40 weeks
medium
Pencil and
watercolour
purpose of work
To illustrate the
HEA Pregnancy
Book

brief
To show the baby
in the mother's
womb at 31-40
weeks with basic
anatomy
commissioned by
Susan Jilanee
company/client
Health Education
Authority

chris orr & associates

Royal Mail House
11 Portland Street
Southampton
SO14 7EB

t. 01703 333 991
f. 01703 333 995

title
Petrograd Fortress,
St Petersburg
Street by Street

medium
Line and
watercolour wash

purpose of work
3D aerial
illustration for a
travel guide

brief
Accurate detailed
aerial view of given
area to include
listed sites and
walk routes - visit
site, research and
photograph and
produce illustration
in studio

illustrator
Mark Powell, Adam
Finch and Chris Orr

commissioned by
Marisa Renzullo

company
Dorling Kindersley
Adult

client
Eye Witness Travel
Guides

title
The Kremlin,
Moscow Street by
Street

medium
Line and
watercolour wash

purpose of work
3D aerial
illustration for a
travel guide

brief
Accurate detailed
aerial view of given
area to include
listed sites and
walk routes - visit
site, research and
photograph and
produce illustration
in studio

illustrator
Mark Powell and
Chris Orr

commissioned by
Marisa Renzullo

company
Dorling Kindersley
Adult

client
Eye Witness Travel
Guides

title
Beyoğlu, Istanbul
Street by Street

medium
Line and
watercolour wash

purpose of work
3D aerial
illustration for a
travel guide

brief
Accurate detailed
aerial view of given
area to include
listed sites and
walk routes - visit
site, research and
photograph and
produce illustration
in studio

illustrator
Mike Johnson,
Adam Finch and
Chris Orr

commissioned by
Kate Poole

company
Dorling Kindersley
Adult

client
Eye Witness Travel
Guides

judges

Richard Peach **design director** Conran Design Group
Christopher Corr **illustrator**
Stuart Colville **senior designer** The Ian Logan Company
Angela Porter **creative director** Interbrand Newell & Sorrell

print & design

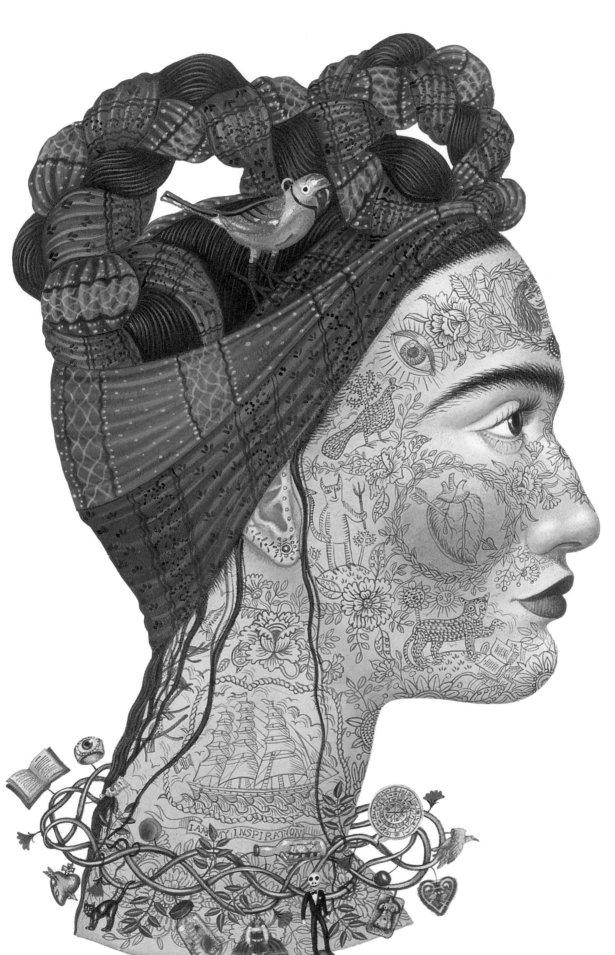

title
I am my Inspiration

medium
Acrylics

purpose of work
Promotion for
Black Book

brief
"I am my
inspiration". A
mailing for the
Black Book Call for
Entries, 1998, USA

commissioned by
Lori McDaniel
company
McDaniel Design
Inc

client
Black Book

agent
Arena
144 Royal College
Street
Camden
London
NW1 oTA
t. 0171 267 9661

ivan allen

The Drawing Room
38 Mount Pleasant
London
WC1X 0AP

t. 0171 713 5489
f. 0171 833 3064

title
Two legged Mutton

medium
Acrylic on acetate

purpose of work
Promotional
calendar

brief
To illustrate fact
that in the Song
dynasty in Ancient
China some
establishments had
human flesh on the
menu, or "Two
legged Mutton"

Commissioned by
Nick Belson

company/client
Origin Design

zafer & barbara baran 47 Kings Road
Richmond
Surrey
TW10 6EG

t. 0181 948 3050
f. 0181 948 3050

title
Christmas Tree

medium
Liquid watercolour
and ink

purpose of work
Christmas-card
illustration

brief
To produce six card
designs with a
humorous twist

commissioned by
Trevor Dunton

company/client
Whistling Fish

stephen bliss

Flat 4
110 Edith Grove
London
SW10 0NH

t. 0171 352 7686
f. 0171 376 8727

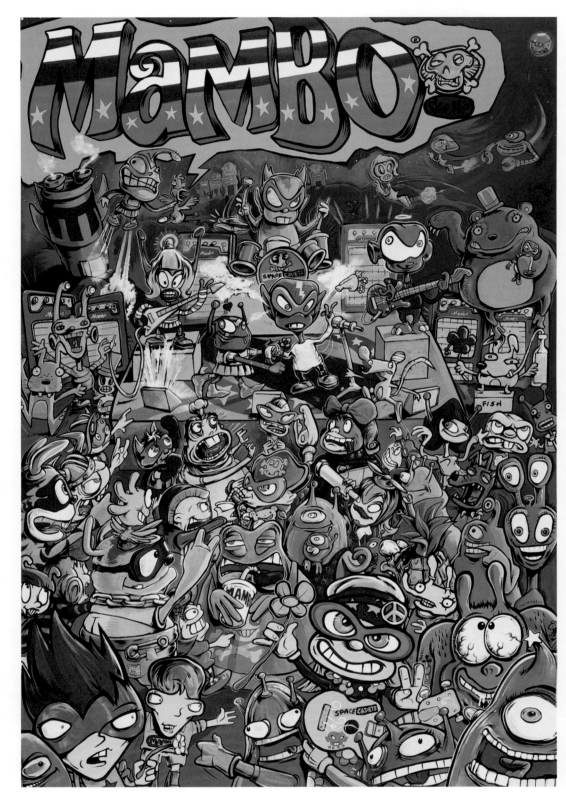

title
Return to the
Planet of the Space
Cadets

medium
Acrylic and ink

purpose of work
Poster for Mambo
fashion label,
children's range

brief
Produce a poster
to entertain and
intrigue kids - a
rock concert in
space

commissioned by
Mark Tydeman

company/client
Mambo UK

kirsten leonora burke   29 Lizban Street
Blackheath
London
SW3 8SS

t. 0181 853 5037
f. 0181 858 6409

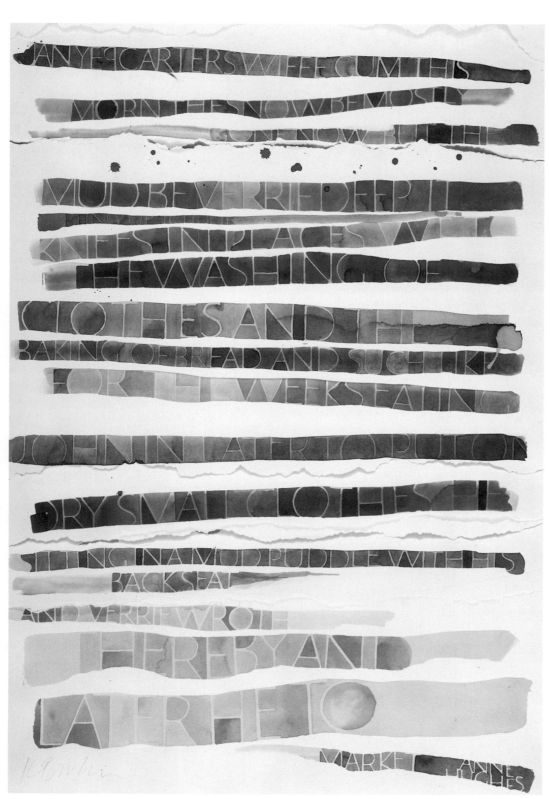

title
Diary of a Farmer's
wife

medium
Food colour on
printing paper

purpose of work
Enhance image of
client and artist

brief
An exhibition of
modern calligraphy
with the theme
"Food and Drink"
to tour selected
branches of All Bar
One

commissioned by
Jeremy Spencer

company/client
All Bar One

jill calder

20 Henderson Street
Flat 3F2
Leith
Edinburgh
EH6 6BS

t. 0131 553 2986
f. 0131 553 2986
email: Jill.C@btinternet.com

152
GB

title
Beer Shopping

medium
Ink

purpose of work
How supermarkets
have the upper
hand in the alcohol
retail market

brief
To depict a
supermarket aisle
full of beer

commissioned by
Andrew Lindsay /
Steve Drummond

company
The Union
Advertising Agency

client
Scottish Courage
Brands Limited

title
Cochise

medium
Ink and pastels

purpose of work
Illustration for
menu cover

brief
To produce a
colour drawing of
an American Indian
warrior, and other
drawings/lettering
connected to that
era

commissioned by
Lucy Richards

company
Lucy Richards
Design

client
Cochise Restaurant

michael clark

60 St John's Grove
London
N19 5RP

t. 0171 272 8943
f. 0171 272 8943

title	brief
A Little Taste of Normandy	To design a birthday card and wrapping paper
medium	
Watercolour on paper	**commissioned by** Julia Woodmansterne
purpose of work	**company/client**
Birthday card / wrapping paper	Woodmansterne Publications Ltd

sarah coleman

71 Rose Cottages
Factory Road
Hinckley
Leicestershire
LE10 0DW

t. 01455 632819
f. 01455 632819
www.AOI.co.uk

154
GB

title
The Twelve Days of Christmas

medium
3D / Mixed

purpose of work
Illustration for cover of company Christmas card

brief
A colourful but elegant image to reference the starry nature of the clients on Billy Marsh's books, without resorting to tired Christmas or theatrical imagery

commissioned by
Jan Kennedy

company
Billy Marsh Associates Theatrical Agency

linda combi

17 Albemarle Road
York
YO23 1EW

t. 01904 623036
f. 01904 623036

title
Lion Splash

medium
Bromide of Splash,
pen and ink, then
silkscreen

purpose of work
Part of a paper
samples booklet

brief
The theme of the
booklet was
"anything you want
it to be".
Illustrators were
asked to interpret
and draw into an
ink splash

commissioned by
Peter Silk

company
Silk/Pearce

client
Arjo Wiggins

nelly dimitranova

Top Flat
33 Savernake Road
London
NW3 2JU

t. 0171 284 2334

title
The Orange Seller
medium
Acrylic and crayon
purpose of work
Poster

brief
To capture the
atmosphere of
Zanzibar market.
Drawing from a
recent trip to Africa
commissioned by
Licenced by Art
Angels

company
Published by
Graphique de
France
client
Christopher
Cordingley

title
Zanzibary Fruit
medium
Acrylic
purpose of work
Poster

brief
Zanzibary fruit
inspired from a
recent trip to
Zanzibar
commissioned by
Licenced by Art
Angels

company
Published by
Graphique de
France
client
Christopher
Cordingley

title
Spring into 98
medium
Acrylic and crayon
purpose of work
Illustration for the
magazine's spring
mailing
brief
Spring 98 for the
English Heritage
commissioned by
Yuriko Kishida
company
Heritage Today

elena gomez

Stonelands
Portsmouth Road
Milford
Surrey
GN8 5DR

t. 01483 423 876
f. 01483 423 935

157

GB

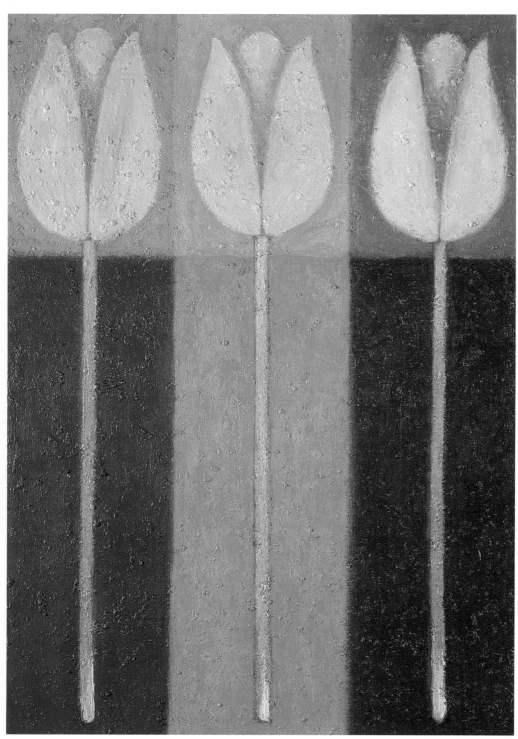

title
Tulip March
medium
Acrylic
purpose of work
Card design
brief
Floral card design
commissioned by
Janie Markham
company/client
The Art Group

christopher gunson

63 Sudbury Court
Allen Edwards
Drive
London
SW8 2NT

t. 0171 622 7559

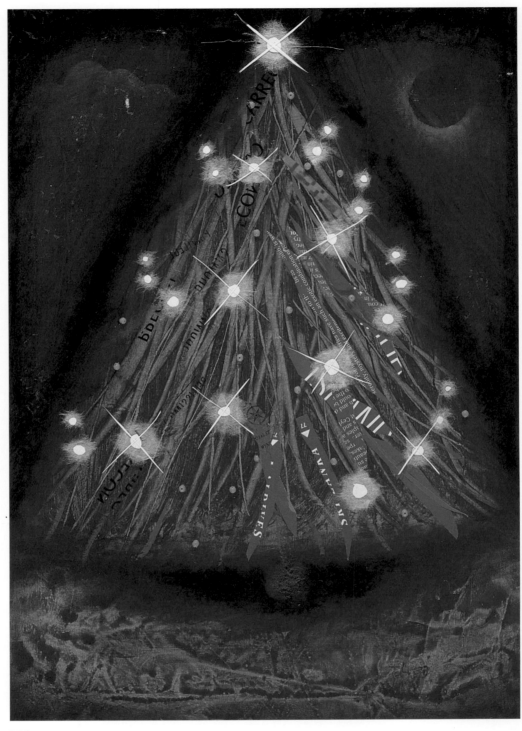

title
Christmas Tree

medium
Mixed media

purpose of work
Christmas card

brief
Open brief to
produce a card
design suitable for
Amnestys (British
section)
Christmas
catalogue

commissioned by
Amnesty
International

jon d hamilton

No 1 Bickley Road
London
E10 7AQ

t. 0181 556 3757
f. 0181 926 3029
pager. 01523 446 401

159

GB

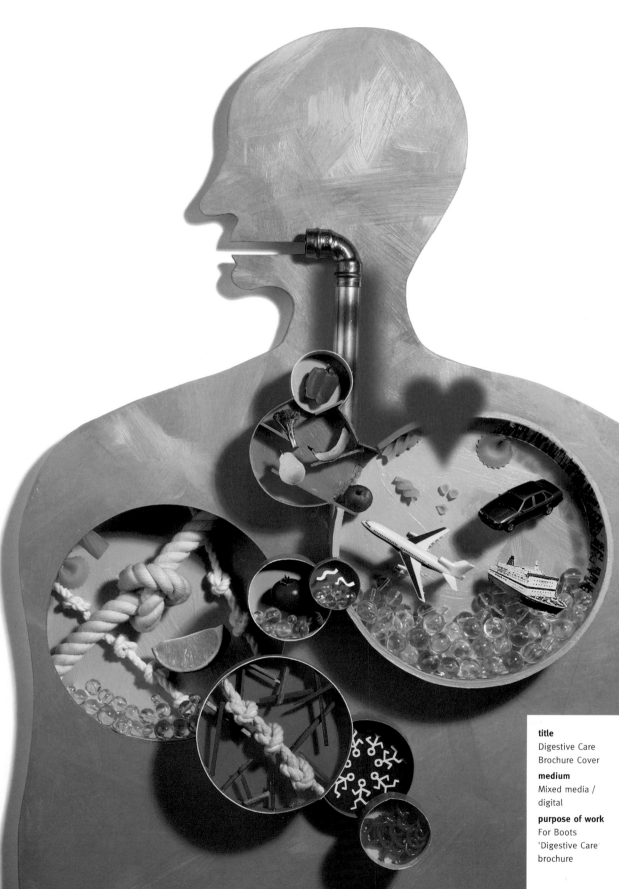

title
Digestive Care
Brochure Cover

medium
Mixed media /
digital

purpose of work
For Boots
'Digestive Care'
brochure

brief
To illustrate front
cover of Boots
'Digestive Care'
brochure showing a
wide range of
situations - travel
sickness, wind,
constipation etc in
a friendly and fun
way, yet
informative

commissioned by
Boots Design
Services

company
Boots

client
Tracey Moult

sara hayward

Four Seasons
74 Battenhall
Avenue
Worcester
WR5 2HW

t. 01905 357563
f. 01905 357563

title
Diet and Arthritis

medium
Acrylic

purpose of work
Booklet

brief
'Produce an
illustration for a
booklet on diet
and arthritis

commissioned by
Keir Windsor

company/client
Arthritis Research
Campaign

ciaran hughes

33 Reservoir Road
London
SE4 2NU

t. 0171 771 0615
f. 0171 771 0615
e-mail. thebhoys@dircon.co.uk

title
Surfing the Net

medium
Digital

purpose of work
Accompany an
in-house guide on
the Internet

brief
Series of
illustrations on
Internet use:
Clockwise from top
left - Getting
Started, Deadlines,
Q&A, Passwords,
Creating your own
Page, Training
Temps

commissioned by
Iva Schroeder

company
Schroeder
Communications

client
Abbey National

curtis jobling

25 Thetford Road
Great Sankey
Warrington
WA5 3EQ

t. 01925 722591
f. 01925 728468

162
GB

title
Fishbone
medium
Acrylic
purpose of work
Animation and
Greetings Card
concept
brief
Concept design for
puppet animated
series and range of
greeting cards

satoshi kambayashi

Flat 2
40 Tisbury Road
Hove
East Sussex
BN3 3BA

t. 01273 771539
f. 01273 771539

title	**commissioned by**
The Last Tree	Mike Dempsey
medium	**company**
India Ink and	CDT
watercolour	**client**
purpose of work	RSA
A full page	**agent**
illustration for RSA	Ian Fleming
Journal	72-74 Brewer
brief	Street
Corporate sector	London
does have to think	WIR 3PH
about the	t. 0171 734 8701
environment now -	
green tax may be	
the answer	

164
GB

title
Four Doctor Types

medium
Indian Ink

purpose of work
Illustration to article
in the Atticus File

brief
A market research
project that
showed how
doctors can be
classified as four
types

commissioned by
David Freeman

company
Enterprise / IG

client
WPP Group plc

title
Find the Animals

medium
Wood Engraving

purpose of work
Illustration in a
paper swatch book

brief
Show that by
looking more
closely, one will
find the illustration,
like the paper it's
printed on, offers
more than meets
the eye

commissioned by
James Hewitt /
David Freeman

company
Enterprise / IG

client
Sappi Europe

Account Director
Anita Macdonald

agent
The Artworks
70 Rosaline Road
London
SW6 7QT
t. 0171 610 1801

clare mackie

21a Ursula Street
London
SW11 3DW

t. 0171 223 8649
f. 0171 223 4119

166

GB

title
Happy Christmas

medium
Watercolour and
ink

purpose of work
Christmas card for
clients

brief
To produce a
Christmas card
suitable for
Matches clients

commissioned by
Ruth Chaplin

company/client
Matches

agent
Eileen McMahon
& Co
PO Box 1062
Bayonne
NY 07002 USA
t.001 201 436 4362

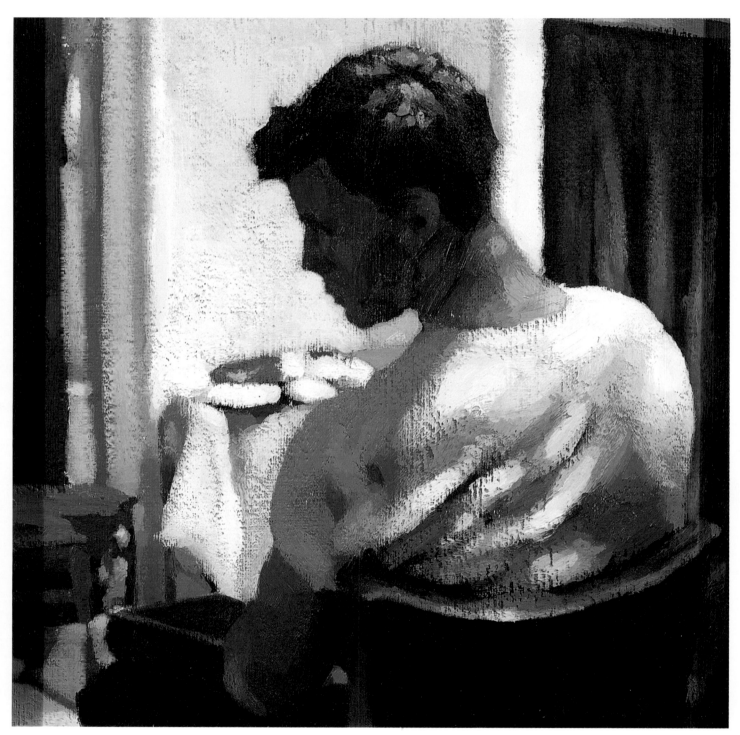

title	commissioned by
The Journal	Claire Ward
medium	**company**
Acrylic on paper	Transworld
purpose of work	**agent**
For inclusion on	The Inkshed
brochure for	98 Columbia Road
Waterstones / Black	London
Swan Illustration	E2 7QB
Competition	t. 0171 613 2323

brief
To produce a
painting which
incorporates the
letter 'W'

james marsh

21 Elms Road
London
SW4 9ER

t. 0171 622 9530
f. 0171 498 6851

GB

title
Strategic Alliances
medium
Acrylic on canvas
purpose of work
Cover of brochure

brief
Open brief for
subject about
banks looking for
ways to expand
their capabilities by
finding the right
partners
commissioned by
John Robertson
company
Robertson Design
Inc
client
Bank Director

title
Philosophy is
Clarity
medium
Acrylic on canvas
purpose of work
Promotional -
brochure

brief
To illustrate the
title for a
management
brochure promotion
commissioned by
Bhandari Design,
Canada
company/client
The Pinnacle Group

maggy milner

Home Farm Cottage
Westhorpe
Southwell
NG25 0NG

t. 01636 814987 / 041 051 5699
f. 01636 814987

title
Infertility

medium
Photographic
multi-image to
transparency

purpose of work
Front cover/book
jacket for the
Infertility
Companion

brief
One in six women
are infertile - use
clinical colours and
props with eggs
and flower, one
egg broken

commissioned by
Amanda McKlevie

company
Harper Collins

aileen mitchell

30H Rowley Way
London
NW8 0SQ

t. 0171 328 8671
f. 0171 328 8180

170

GB

title
Dream Garden II
medium
Watercolour and
gouache
purpose of work
One of six posters
for children's
rooms

brief
Adapt book idea of
boy dreaming from
bed to landscape -
via bedspread.
Make six images
which work
separately and
together
commissioned by
Hans Kunz

company/client
Wizard & Genius

ian murray

10 Essex Avenue
Dibsbury
Manchester
M20 6AN

t. 0161 448 0260
f. 0161 448 8504

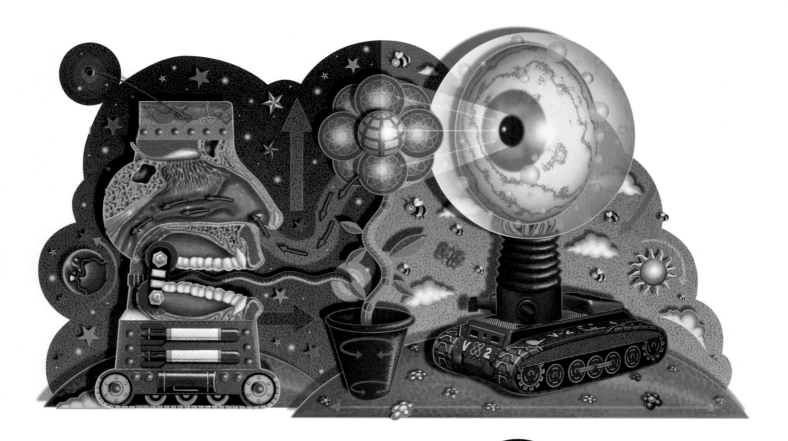

title
Sight and Smel

medium
Computer
generated

purpose of work
Illustrations for
software
consultancy
brochure

brief
Illustrate the way
in which the use of
business software
will encourage the
growth of a new
business

commissioned by
Blue Bark

client
Axiom

title
Future Shock

medium
Computer
generated

purpose of work
Illustrations for
software
consultancy
brochure

brief
Illustrate how
business software
can help the client
predict business
trends in the future

commissioned by
Blue Bark

client
Axiom

sarah perkins

37e Guinness Court
Snowfields
London
SE1 3SX

t. 0171 378 1510
f. 0171 357 6442

title
White Wine
medium
Mixed
purpose of work
Wine label

brief
Free - but feeling of
lightness, delicacy,
pale
commissioned by
Ernesto Aparicio
company
E. Aparicio Design
client
Domaine Saint-
Amant
agent
The Inkshed
98 Columbia Road
London E2 7QB

ingram pinn

33 Alexandra Road
London
W4 1AX

t. 0181 994 5311
f. 0181 747 8200

GB

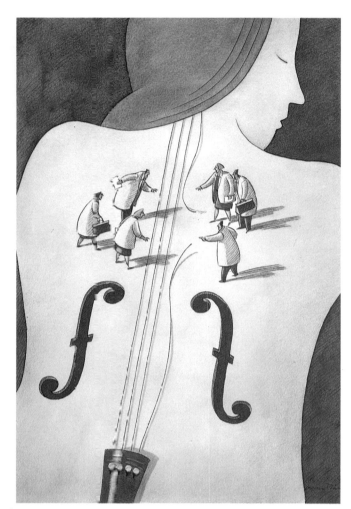 

title	**brief**	**title**	**brief**
Spinal Cord Injuries	To Illustrate a	Alzheimer's	To illustrate a
medium	poster promoting a	**medium**	poster offering a
Ink, watercolour	conference on	Ink, watercolour	grant for research
and crayon	spinal cord injuries	and crayon	into Alzheimer's
purpose of work	**commissioned by**	**purpose of work**	disease
Poster	Gabriel Maillard	Poster	**commissioned by**
	company		Jacqueline
	IRME, Paris		Mervaillie
			company
			Fondation Ipsen,
			Paris

ian pollock

GB

171 Bond Street
Macclesfield
Cheshire
SK11 6RE

t. 01625 426205
f. 01625 261390

title
Bernard Manning
medium
Watercolour ink
and gouache
purpose of work
Part of title
sequence for BBC
North's "The Big
Question"

brief
Portrait of Bernard
Manning
commissioned by
BBC North
company/client
BBC North
agent
The Inkshed
98 Columbia Road
London
E2 7QB
t. 0171 613 2323

paul powis

Four Seasons
74 Battenhall
Avenue
Worcester
WR5 2HW

t. 01905 357563
f. 01905 357563

GB

title
Golden Valley
medium
Acrylic
purpose of work
Poster print

brief
To produce a lively
painterly landscape
commissioned by
Dominic Seckleer
company
Nouvelle Images

michael sheehy

115 Crystal Palace
Road
East Dulwich
London
SE22 9ES

t. 0181 693 4315
f. 0181 693 4315

title
Plain Chocolate
Espresso Beans

medium
Watercolour

purpose of work
Coffee Bean
Packaging

brief
Create a character
for a flavoured
coffee bean to
appear on
packaging

commissioned by
Lindsey Turnham

company
Ian Logan Design

client
Whittards of
Chelsea

title
Double Chocolate
Truffle

medium
Watercolour

purpose of work
Coffee Bean
Packaging

brief
Create a character
for a flavoured
coffee bean to
appear on
packaging

commissioned by
Lindsey Turnham

company
Ian Logan Design

client
Whittards of
Chelsea

michael terry

12 Bartholomew Street
Hythe
Kent
CT21 5BS

t. 01303 269456
f. 01303 269456
http. www.illustrator.org.uk/big/ilstrtrs/terry

title
Badger's Watch

medium
Gouache and
coloured pencil

purpose of work
Inn Sign for
Vintage Inns

brief
To humorously
illustrate the name
"Badger's Watch"

commissioned by
Mike Tisdale

company
Sign Specialists Ltd

client
Vintage Inns

peter till

178

GB

11 Berkeley Road
London
N8 8RU

t. 0181 341 0497
f. 0181 341 0497

title
New York Bottle

medium
Pen, ink and
watercolour

purpose of work
Brochure
illustration

brief
Image of Macallan
in New York

commissioned by
Andrew Wolffe

company
Tayburn McIlroy
Coates

client
Macallan

russell walker

9 Sussex Road
Colchester
Essex
CO3 3QH

t. 01206 577766

GB

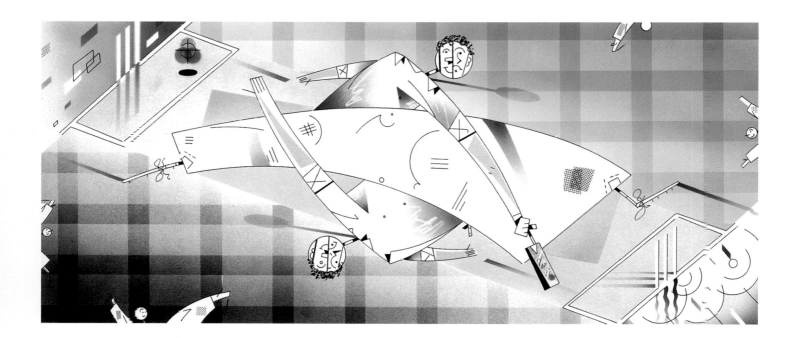

title
Run Em Up,
Run Im Out

medium
Ink

purpose of work
Contribution to
1998 Calendar

brief
To produce an
image that reflects
time of year, and
introduces the
theme of Paper
and Flint

commissioned by
Douglas McArthur

client
Caledonian Paper

judges

Paul Slater **illustrator**
John Hughes **agent** London Art Collection
Dominic Finnigan **senior designer** Spy Design
Michael Mascaro **designer** Random House
Philip Davies **partner** Creative Partnership Marketing

student

stephen waterhouse

2a Norwood Grove
Birkenshaw
Bradford
West Yorkshire
BD11 2NP

t. 01274 877111
f. 01274 877111

182

GB

title
The Bird Market

medium
Acrylic

purpose of work
Book written and
illustrated for the
Macmillan
Children's book
prize

brief
To create
illustrations with an
emphasis on the
appeal of the work
to children, strong
colour, good
composition skills
and an ability to
match pictures with
text

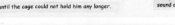

... and grow ...

until the cage could not hold him any longer.

Grasping his chance for freedom, he made a joyful
sound and flapped his wings towards the other birds.

As the cool breeze rustled the leaves and the clear
moon touched the sea, the baby toucan danced on
the rooftops and waved goodbye to the birdseller.

They flew the bird seller to a land far far away.
Finally free from their cages, the birds made
new lives for themselves on islands of their own.
Just as God had intended.

On an island far out at sea, there was a special
market, and people travelled to it from far and near.

stephen waterhouse

2a Norwood Grove
Birkenshaw
Bradford
West Yorkshire
BD11 2NP

t. 01274 877111
f. 01274 877111

title
The High, Winding
Road to
Valldemossa in
Majorca

medium
Acrylic

purpose of work
Advertising

brief
To create an image
with warm vibrant
colours and a
diverse
composition, for
use upon a travel
brochure,
advertising trips
around the Balearic
islands

title
A Willingness to
Play is a Pre-
condition to
Creativity

medium
Mixed Media

purpose of work
Self promotional -
Development from
Editorial

brief
To explore the
transformation from
two dimensional
imagery to low
relief, with an
emphasis on form,
texture and design

title
Learning to Dance

medium
Acrylic

purpose of work
A series of
illustrations for a
children's book

brief
To produce a
number of spot
illustrations for a
book about the
relationships
between mothers
and their children

stephen waterhouse

2a Norwood Grove
Birkenshaw
Bradford
West Yorkshire
BD11 2NP

t. 01274 877111
f. 01274 877111

184

GB

title
The Mardi Gras Jazz
Festival

medium
Mixed Media

purpose of work
Advertising

brief
To produce a three
dimensional
moving model, to
advertise this
prestigious event,
using a diversity of
shape, size, form
and media.

richard calvert

Cheltenham and Gloucester
College of Higher Education

Little Beech Oast
Penhurst
Nr Battle
East Sussex
TN33 9QS

t. 01424 772883
f. 01424 775156

title
Kitchen Table
Discussion

medium
Acrylic and paint
stik on canvas

purpose of work
Personal
promotional work

brief
To portray a
relationship,
perhaps
relationships ir
general

title
The Day the Earth
Stood Still

medium
Acrylic and paint
stik on canvas

purpose of work
Personal
promotional work

brief
To illustrate how
callously we treat
our precious
natural resources

jonathan cusick

10 Wynyates
Sageside,
Tamworth
Staffordshire
B79 7UP

t. 01827 50003
f. 01827 50003

title
The Three Wise
Men
medium
Acrylics
purpose of work
Christmas card

brief
To produce a
seasonal card while
suggesting
directions available
in art education at
Birmingham
Institute of Art and
Design
tutors
Andrew Kulman &
Patrick Mortemore
University of
Central England in
Birmingham

title
Old Tractors and
the Men who Love
them
medium
Acrylics & ink
purpose of work
Book jacket

brief
To produce a cover
for a book titled
"Old Tractors and
the Men who Love
them"
tutors
Andrew Kulman &
Patrick Mortemore
University of
Central England in
Birmingham

title
Ouch !
medium
Acrylics
purpose of work
Hasbro advertising
('Operation')

brief
To create
emotional exciting
images of multi-
cultural consumers
using Hasbro toy
products. The
images should
reflect the Hasbro
strapline "We make
fun for everyone"
tutors
Andrew Kulman &
Patrick Mortemore
University of
Central England in
Birmingham

jonathan cusick

10 Wynyates
Sageside,
Tamworth
Staffordshire
B79 7UP

t. 01827 50003
f. 01827 50003

title
Once there were
Two

medium
Acrylics

purpose of work
Self promotional

brief
Illustrate an article
about the lone twin
network

tutors
Andrew Kulman
University of
Central England in
Birmingham

jonathan cusick

10 Wynyates
Sageside,
Tamworth
Staffordshire
B79 7UP

t. 01827 50003
f. 01827 50003

188
GB

title
The King's
Instrument

medium
Acrylics

purpose of work
Self promotional

brief
To represent Elvis
Presley in an
inventive and
original way

tutors
Andrew Kulman
University of
Central England in
Birmingham

tim etheridge

Brookside
Plaistow Road
Kirdford
West Sussex
RH14 0NG

t. 01403 820458
pager. 0839 035211
e-mail. T_ETHERIDGE@hotmail.com

189
GB

title
Ned with eyes in
the back of his
head

medium
Acrylic and collage

purpose of work
Student work

brief
To accompany a
poetry piece

title
Billy the King

medium
Acrylic and collage

purpose of work
MacMillan Prize

brief
To illustrate a 32
page children's
book

275

STUDENTS

warwick fraser-coombe

16 Edensor Gardens
Chiswick
London
W4 2QY

t. 07970 179188 /
0181 580 1783

title
Quicksands:
Hunter Head

medium
Mixed media on
canvas

purpose of work
Book jacket /
poster

brief
Book jacket for
graphic novel

title
Executioner

medium
Mixed media on
card

purpose of work
Book jacket

brief
Book jacket for
"Death in the
Falklands"

samuel hearn

6 Popham Gardens
Lower Richmond Road
Richmond
Surrey
TW9 4LJ

t. 0181 878 7453
mobile. 0958 966 218

title
A staple diet for
the overweight
medium
Drawing on acetate
purpose of work
Project at
University
brief
Article on stapling
stomachs
agent
Eastwing
98 Columbia Road
London
E2 7QB
t. 0171 613 5580

title
Joint Custody
medium
Drawing on acetate
purpose of work
Project at
University
brief
Article on life as a
butcher's son
agent
Eastwing
98 Columbia Road
London
E2 7QB
t. 0171 613 5580

richard johnson

30 Glen Way
Oadby
Leicester
LE2 5YE

t. 0116 271 3891

title
Murder

medium
Acrylic

purpose of work
College Project

brief
Taking life room
work into a studio
based project

title
Death in the Family

medium
Acrylic

purpose of work
College Project

brief
Studio project -
editorial

sarah lockwood

16 Christine Close
Bexhill-on-Sea
East Sussex
TN40 2RJ

t. 01424 222666

title
Scrooge and Marley
medium
Coloured pencil,
white acrylic paint
purpose of work
Interior illustrations
for Charles Dickens'
'A Christmas Carol'

brief
To produce a series
of images for 'A
Christmas Carol'
which capture the
mood and setting
of the story

saeko matsushita

c/o Furukata
13 rue Ernest Cresson
Paris 75014
France

t. 0033 1 45 43 38 17
e-mail. raizo_n@yahoo.com

title
The Sound of the
wind blowing,
howling and
wuthering

medium
Etching and
aquatint,
watercolour

purpose of work
College work for
final assessment

brief
From the series of
imaginary drawings
based on my own
fairy tales

title
In the Cafè - Can I
have sugar cubes?

medium
Computer
generated

purpose of work
College work for
final assessment

brief
From the series of
imaginary drawings
based on my own
dreams

eva tatcheva

80 Waverley Road
Harrow
Middlesex
HA2 9RD

t. 0181 866 3586
f. 0181 866 3586

GB

title
Piece of Cake
medium
Mixed media
purpose of work
Illustration for
article about the
diversity of young
European chefs

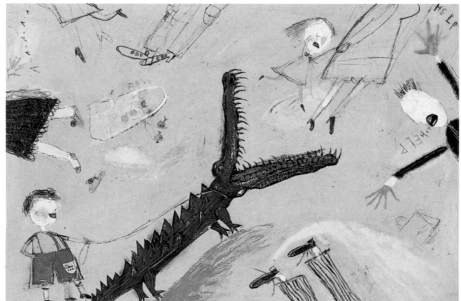

title
If I had a real
crocodile, I would
scare everybody
medium
Mixed media
purpose of work
Children's Book:
'Crocodile Friend'

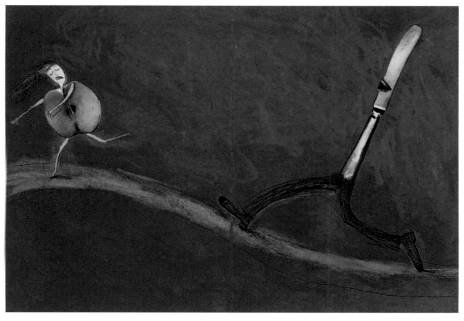

title
Forbidden Fruit
medium
Mixed media
purpose of work
Illustration for an
article on food and
sex

chitra uthaiah

41 Pearl Street
Bedminster
Bristol
BS3 3DZ

t. 0117 902 9460
e-mail. chitra_66@hotmail.com

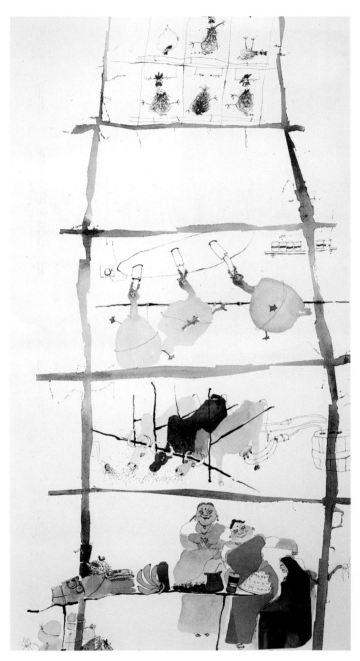

title
Pâte de Fois Gras
medium
Pen and ink and
watercolour
purpose of work
Self promotional
study for end of
year show
brief
Examining the role
of Hindu women in
Indian society

title
Luxuriant hair is
necessary for
breeding many
children
medium
Pen and ink and
watercolour

purpose of work
Self promotional
study for end of
year show
brief
Examining the role
of Hindu women in
Indian society

title
Tilts
medium
Pen and ink and
watercolour
purpose of work
Self promotional
study for end of
year show
brief
To produce a
children's book

neil wainwright

6B The Drive
Walthamstow
London
E17 3BW

t. 0181 520 9617
f. 0181 520 9617

197
GB

title
Metropolis
medium
Graphite stick and
pencil
purpose of work
Editorial

brief
The C ty is a
hyperbole of
industry and wealth
but poverty is s ill
widespread

title
The Drive with Milz
Millie
medium
Lino cut
purpose of work
Publishing - book
illustration
brief
To produce
illustrations for
"The Colour
Purple" by Alice
Walker

title
Chicken Flu
medium
Lino cut
purpose of work
Editorial
brief
To accompany an
article discussing
the rise of chicken
flu in Hong Kong

283

mark ward

8 Clements Court
Green Lane
Hounslow
Middlesex
TW4 6EB

t. 0181 577 0308

198
GB

title
Books
medium
Watercolour
purpose of work
Self promotional
brief
Self initiated
project - one of a
series of headings
for a listings
magazine

title
Music
medium
Watercolour
purpose of work
Self promotional
brief
Self initiated
project - one of a
series of headings
for a listings
magazine

annette west

c/o 6 Newham Close
Rothwell
Northamptonshire
NN14 6TT

t. 01536 710516
pager. 01523 770446

title
Fool to be Lost in
Thought

medium
Oil pastel, pencil,
collage

purpose of work
MA Project

brief
An illustration
created in response
to the following
urban haiku poem
by Nigel Young:
Fool to be lost in
thought the military
plane swoops low
and scalps me

olivia williams

12 Clarke Street
Market
Harbourough
Leicestershire
LE16 9AD

t. 01858 446218

200
GB

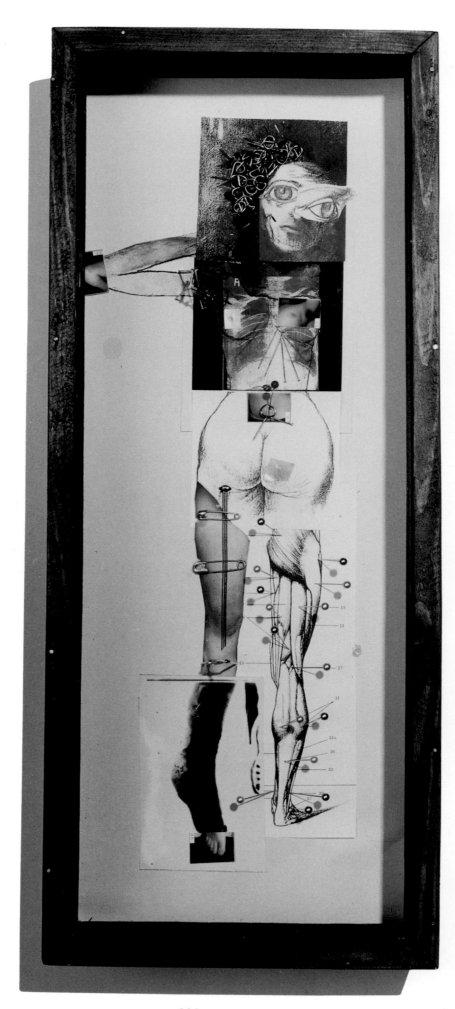

title
Enetophobia
medium
Mixed media
(photocopies/photo
graphs)
purpose of work
Final year projects

brief
To illustrate the
phobia of pins

sam wilson

Cranford
St Nicolas Avenue
Cranleigh
Surrey
GU6 7AQ

t. 01483 274602
f. 01483 274602

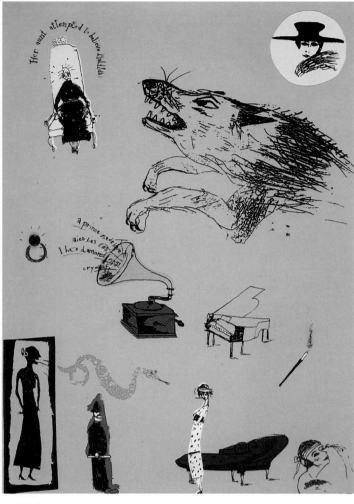

title
Matilda who told lies

medium
Screen print and collage

purpose of work
Self promotional

brief
To introduce the character, Matilda, for a short story book by Hillaire Belloc

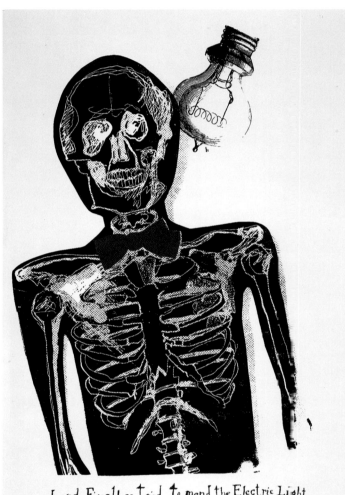

title
Little Suck-a-thumb

medium
Mixed media

purpose of work
Self promotional

brief
To illustrate the moral tale of Little Suck a Thumb by Dr Heinrich Hoffman

title
Lord Finchley

medium
Screen print and collage

purpose of work
Self promotional

brief
To illustrate the moral tale of Lord Finchley by Hillaire Belloc

paula wyatt

Stockers Farm
Stockers Farm Road
Richmansworth
Hertfordshire
WD3 1NZ

t. 01923 773763
f. 01923 773763

202
GB

title
"And 3 cats
appeared"

medium
Monoprint

purpose of work
Macmillan's
Children's Book
competition

brief
Joe bangs on a tin
with a fork and
three cats
appeared

title
"Breakfast"

medium
Monoprint

purpose of work
Macmillan's
Children's Book
competition

brief
Thomas is not
impressed when
the pigs talk with
their mouths full

stuart rowbottom

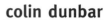

The Grange
Haycroft Lane
Fleet
Nr. Holbeach
Spalding
Lincs
PE12 8LB

t. 01 06 424005

title
Ford Puma

medium
Digital: Illustrator
and Photoshop

purpose of work
Degree project
work

brief
Promotional
poster:
professional brief

submitted by
Blackpool and The
Fylde College

colin dunbar

Flat 3f1
34 Barony Street
Edinburgh
EH3 6NY

t.   131 558 1775

title
Landing Point:
Earth Beach

medium
Oil

purpose of work
Self promotional

brief
To illustrate and
write a story about
an alien's
perceptions of
earth

david mair

ee Agent

title
Girl Holding a Ball

medium
Inks, watercolour
and digital

purpose of work
Learning to use
Photoshop

brief
Self promotional

agent
Sylvie Poggio
31 Crouch Hall
Road
London
N8 8HH
t. 0181 341 2722
f. 0181 374 4753

richard myers

204
GB

13 Cavendish
Avenue
Harrogate
North Yorkshire
HG2 8HX

t. 01423 504172

title
Select and Save by
Night
medium
Charcoal, paint,
collage
purpose of work
Self Promotional
brief
Illustrating on the
theme of
Cambridge at night

graham samuels

52 Abbey Road
Hullbridge
Hockley
Essex
SS5 6DJ

t. 01702 230296

title
Groupie
medium
Acrylic on board
purpose of work
Self promotional
brief
An illustration for
the front cover of
Groupie, a novel by
Jenny Fabian and
Johnny Byrne

nikki tadd

53 Home Ground
Westbury on Trym
Bristol
BS9 4UD

t. 0117 983 3982
pager.
04325 721281

title
Maudlin
medium
Oil paint, thread,
muslin
purpose of work
To illustrate the
poem 'Maudlin' by
Sylvia Plath
brief
Part of a series of
nine illustrations to
accompany poems
by Sylvia Plath in
the form of a book,
where importance is
placed on conveying
the emotions and
thoughts of the
poetry through the
use of colour and
space

nicola taylor

2 Riffams Drive
Basildon
Essex
SS3 1BG

t. 01268 470531
mobile.
0775 668988

title
Feeding Time
medium
Colour pencil
purpose of work
Image for Oxfam
(Not commissioned)
brief
To illustrate an
Oxfam update
article, helping
people to help
themselves

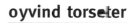

laura madeleine thomas

Flat 4
26 Fore Street
Heavitree
Exeter, Devon
EX1 2RS

t. 01392 253214

title
Jack in the Box
medium
Lino-cut
purpose of work
BA Hons Degree
brief
Illustrations to
accompany
selected short
stories by Ray
Bradbury

oyvind torseter

224 Vestbugdveien
2312 Ottestad
Norway

t. + 47 918 08095

title
Me. In my room
medium
Computer
generated
purpose of work
College work for
final assessment
brief
A drawing of
imaginary space
exploration of inner
landscape

rupert van wyk

130 Bethnal Green
Road
London
E2 6DG

t. 0171 613 3149

title
Colours of India
medium
Pencil, acrylics,
pastels, water
colour
purpose of work
Self promotional
brief
To show some of
the vibrancy and
colour found in
India

sarah willshaw

Knowle Top
Reapsmoor
Nr Longnor
Buxton
Derbyshire
SK17 0LL

t. 01298 84659

title
The Fall of
Patriarchy
medium
Etching and
aquatint print
purpose of work
A cover image for a
book of
contemporary
feminist fairy tales
brief
To produce an
image which
reflects the
changing social
position of women
in a previously
masculine
dominated society

helen wiseman

Pinkneys Manor
Wimbish
Saffron Walden
Essex
CB10 2XD

t. 01799 599788
f. 01799 599788

title
Padstow Harbour
medium
Water colour and
pen
purpose of work
Editorial /
publishing
brief
Reportage project:
illustrate the camel
trail in Cornwall

judges

Ann Howeson **illustrator**

Janet Slingsby **director** Tucker Slingsby

Sheri Safran **director** Tango Books

David Eldridge **director** The Senate

Brian Love **course leader, illustration** Kingston University

unpublished

jill calder

20 Henderson Street
Flat 3F2
Leith
Edinburgh
EH6 6BS

t. 0131 553 2986
f. 0131 553 2986
email: Jill.C@btinternet.com

★ **unpublished section winner**

210

GB

title
Urban Garden No 1

medium
Ink, Acrylic

purpose of work
Personal work
inspired by a trip
to New York City

jill calder

20 Henderson Street
Flat 3F2
Leith
Edinburgh
EH6 6BS

t. 0131 553 2986
f. 0131 553 2986
email: Jill.C@btinternet.com

211

GB

title
Saguaro Wine
medium
Ink
purpose of work
Self promotional -
experimental

sarah black

11 Poplar Avenue
Gorleston
Gt. Yarmouth
Norfolk
NR31 7PW

t. 0966 392040 /
01493 442521
f. 01493 602854

title
Japanese Cookery

medium
Oil bar, gouache,
acrylic, collage

purpose of work
Idea for cookery
book cover based
on types of
cooking

brief
Self promotional
project

title
China

medium
Oil bar, gouache,
acrylic, collage

purpose of work
Ideas for travel or
language guides

brief
Self promotional
project

stephen bliss

Flat 4
110 Edith Grove
London
SW10 0NH

t. 0171 352 7686
f. 0171 376 8727

title
Fish and Chips -
You Don't Need
Drugs
medium
Acrylic on canvas
purpose of work
Self promotional -
experimental
brief
To loosen up, get
away from my
detailed paintings,
have fun

title
Kids are OK
medium
Biro, collage,
Illustrator 6 on
MAC
purpose of work
Self promotional -
experimental
brief
To try a new style
for new portfolio of
computer
generated work

nicholas borden

c/o Lower Bowbier Farm
Bampton
Tiverton
Devon EX16 9EE

t. 01398 331587
mobile. 0958 640 9360
Pager. 01523 148966

214
GB

title
Public Library
Reading
medium
Mixed media
purpose of work
Self promotional

brief
To produce an
unconventional
light-hearted image
to a subject
traditionally
thought of as
rather ordinary

title
Revenge of
Domestic
Technology
medium
Mixed media
purpose of work
Self promotional

brief
To produce an
unconventional
humorous image of
something
generally
considered ordinary

title
Pets who look like
their owners
medium
Mixed media
purpose of work
Self promotional

brief
To consider the
resemblance
between pets and
their owners

michael bramman

104 Dudley Court
Upper Berkeley
Street
London
W1H 7PJ

t. 0171 723 3564
f. 0171 723 3564

title
Blue on Green
medium
Acrylic
purpose of work
Self promotional
brief
Interpretation of
historical
photograph

title
River Boat
medium
Acrylic
purpose of work
Commissioned
sample for hotel
project
brief
Paint river boat -
summer evening

301
.

neil breeden

28 Vere Road
Brighton
East Sussex
BN1 4NR

t. 01273 700857
f. 01273 700857

title
I Dream of Football

medium
Acrylic on wood

purpose of work
Self promotional

brief
The illustrator
sought to recreate
an image of his
lost youth spent on
the playing fields
of Birmingham

hazel natasha brook

9 Mount Pleasant
Crescent
Hastings
East Sussex
TN34 3SG

t. 01424 443541
f. 01424 447770

title
The Shepherd's
Purse

medium
Mixed media

purpose of work
To illustrate a
poem by Elizabeth
Smart

brief
Part of a personal
project to produce
a series of
illustrations to
environmental
poems of the 20th
Century, for a
second book
project

harriet buckley

3F2
4 Buccleuch
Terrace
Edinburgh
EH8 9ND

t. 0131 668 1511
e-mail. harriart@aol.com

title
How they built the
Cutty Sark -
Endpapers
medium
Coloured inks
purpose of work
Self promotional
(self-initiated
picture book)

brief
Endpapers for 32-
page book written
and illustrated by
myself, which
follows each stage
of building the ship
Cutty Sark (keel,
ribs, hull, masts,
sails)

karen burke

Basement Flat
85 St Margarets Road
Twickenham
London TW1 2LJ

pager. 07666 789 435
e-mail. the2burkes@compuserve.com

title
Melon Heaven
medium
Acrylic
purpose of work
Self promotional
brief
To produce an
image that could
be used as a
greetings card

title
Daisy Chain
medium
Acrylic
purpose of work
Self promotional
brief
To produce an
image that could
be used as a
greetings card

UNPUBLISHED

steven carroll

63 Upper Craigour
Edinburgh
EH17 7SE

t. 0131 658 1975
f. 0131 658 1975

220

GB

title
I wanna do Richard
III

medium
Alkyd paints

purpose of work
Experimental Self
promotional

brief
To portray Eddie
Izzard as King
Richard the third; a
role in which he
himself has
expressed an
interest.

grant carruthers

1 Woodburn House
Woodburn Place
St Andrews
Fife KY16 8LA

t. 01334 476866

title
Goodbye To Berlin

medium
Mixed (collage /
3D / photographic /
ink)

purpose of work
Unpublished
personal project

brief
To design a book
jacket for the
Christopher
Isherwood novel
"Goodbye To
Berlin"

simon john davies

16 Leicester
Crescent
Wharf View Road
Ilkley
West Yorkshire
LS29 8DX

t. 01943 608562

222

GB

title
Yorkshire Dales -
wet & cool

medium
Collage

purpose of work
Speculative / Self
Promotional

brief
To present a series
of walks within the
Yorkshire Dales,
charting the
constantly changing
conditions: warm
to cold, wet to dry,
sun to snow

title
That perfect Greek
isle

medium
Acrylic

purpose of work
Speculative / Self
Promotional

brief
A travelogue
exploration seeking
that perfect Greek
isle, via the travel
brochures ("believe
me, this is the
one")

peter davies

36 Lower North
Street
Exeter
EX4 3EU

t. 01392 430174
f. 01392 430174

223

GB

title
Merry-go-round
medium
Mixed media
purpose of work
Self promotional -
greeting cards

brief
Imagery inspired by
travelling
fairgrounds
directed
speculatively
towards the
greeting cards
market

title
The Bandstand
medium
Coloured inks
purpose of work
Self promotional -
greeting cards

brief
From a series
placing figures in
landscape directed
towards the
greeting cards
market

joanne davies

224
GB

36 Lower North
Street
Exeter
EX4 3EU

t. 01392 430174
f. 01392 430174

title
The town crier
announces all
productions of
Topsham Amateur
Dramatic Society
and runs the fish
van

medium
Gouache

purpose of work
MA project
brief
Page from book
based on
characters living in
Topsham village in
Devon

joanne davies

36 Lower North
Street
Exeter
EX4 3EU

t. 01392 430 74
f. 01392 430 74

title
Roy the Dog only
likes going for a
walk in the car

medium
Gouache

purpose of work
MA project

brief
Page from book
based on
characters living in
Topsham village in
Devon

title
Miss Dors has a
bad leg so no man
will have her

medium
Gouache

purpose of work
MA project

brief
Page from book
based on
characters living in
Topsham village in
Devon

nick dewar

UK
Eastwing
98 Columbia Road
London
E27 QB

t. 0171 613 5580
f. 0171 613 2726

USA
Kate Larkworthy
Apt 4D
32 Downing Street
New York 10014

t. 001 212 633 1310
f. 001 212 633 1310

title
Mall Moll

medium
Acrylic

purpose of work
Promotional in USA

heidi donohoe

16 Elle borough Close
Brackm ll
Berksl e
RG12 4B

t. 013 86 631
mobile 077 1 698772

title
Strange Vi tors
medium
Collograph nd
pastel/liqu
purpose of vork
Promotiona Ima e
- editorial latec

brief
To produce an
editorial image that
reflects the
possibility that we
are being visited by
extra-terrestrial life
forms

serena feneziani

53 Finlay Street
London
SW6 6HF

t. 0171 403 1783
f. 0171 403 1783

228
GB

title
Countryside
medium
Watercolour and
pen
purpose of work
Picture of
countryside to be
used as
background

brief
Pop-up book
commissioned by
Sue Tarsky

t. 01348 831831
mobile.07970 623692

title
Global Warming

medium
Acrylic dyes / gouache

purpose of work
Self promotional

brief
To depict a mood of foreboding from the effects of greenhouse gas emissions on the environment, contributing to changing weather patterns and rising sea levels

elena gomez

Stonelands
Portsmouth Road
Milford
Surrey
GN8 5DR

t. 01483 423 876
f. 01483 423 935

230

GB

title
Meadow
medium
Acrylic
purpose of work
Self promotional
brief
Self promotional
piece for print or
card

nicolette green

96 Stanford Avenue
Brighton
East Sussex
BN1 6FE

t. 01273 506875
f. 01273 506875
e-mail. ickies@pavilion.co.uk

231
GB

title
What are those lights Papa Wolf?

medium
Watercolour / bleach / pencil crayon

purpose of work
Double page illustration for a proposed picture book with author Paul Stewart

brief
To show the young wolf's fear of the towering trees, bear shapes in the stars and staring eyes in the dark

317
UNPUBLISHED

brian grimwood

c/o CIA
36 Wellington Street
London WC2

t. 0171 240 8925
www.briangrimwood.com

232
GB

UNPUBLISHED

title
Chinese Landscape

medium
Computer
generated

purpose of work
Presentation for
Disney Promotion

brief
Proposed idea for
stage set

commissioned by
Shane Greeves

company
Enterprise

sally grover

Studio 358
Clerkenwell Workshops
27 Clerkenwell Close
London
EC1R oAT

t. 056 609157
t/f. 0171 336 7053

233

GB

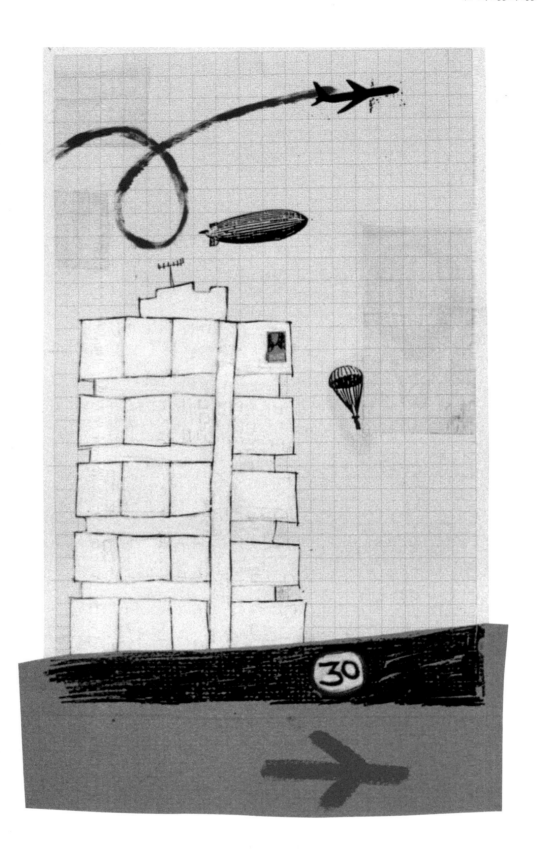

title
Princess Ida

medium
Mixed media

purpose of work
Self promotional -
poster

brief
To illustrate the
opera Princess Ida
by Gilbert &
Sullivan for a
production by the
Royal College of
Music

andrew harris

8a Birdhurst Rise
South Croydon
Surrey
CR2 7ED

t. 0181 681 0310
e-mail. n.anderson@btinternet.com

234
GB

title
Snapping up the
Greenbelt

medium
Woodcut

purpose of work
Self promotional

MAGNET
ARTISTS

Piero (hernan pierini)
5 Bedford House
61 Lisson St
London
NW1 5DD

t. 0171 724 4592
f. 0171 724 4592
e-mail. piero@dial.pipex.com

title
Cook
medium
Watercolour
purpose of work
Cookery brochure

brief
To create
illustrations about
creative cookery
with a touch of
humour, funny
situations

p i e r o

i l l u s t r a t o r

valerie heskins

15 Stratford Court
Westover Gardens
Westbury on Trym
Bristol
BS9 3NE

t. 0117 950 1162
f. 0117 950 1162

236
GB

title
Bra-vo

medium
Coloured pencil

purpose of work
Self promotional

brief
To illustrate an
article on the
technical
innovations in the
history of the bra

sophie joyce

Flat 8
39 St James St
Brighton
East Sussex
BN2 1RG

t. 01273 695626
f. 01273 695626

title
Man and Dog
medium
Pastel
purpose of work
Self promotional

brief
Originally done as a self promotional piece, this image has since been used by Ling Design as part of an occasional and everyday greetings card range

alison lang

Suite 7
24 Warwick Road
London
SW5 9UD

t. 0171 598 1037
f. 0171 598 1037

238
GB

title
The Imperfect
Nanny
medium
Watercolour
purpose of work
Self promotional
brief
To depict Louise
Woodward as Mary
Poppins in a
topical personality
series

The Imperfect Nanny

stewart lees

47 Greevegate
Huntstanton
Norfolk
PE36 6AF

t. 01485 542061
f. 01485 542061

title
Martha
medium
Oils
purpose of work
Self promotional
agent
Folio
10 Gate Street
Lincoln's Inn Fields
London
WC2A 3HP
t. 0171 242 9562

frank love

The Dairy
5-7 Marischal Road
London
SE13 5LE

t. 0181 297 2212
f. 0181 297 2212

title
City Dogs
medium
Mixed media
purpose of work
Self promotional

brief
A business image
without little
people doing big
things together
agency
Eastwing
98 Columbia Road
London
E2 7QB
t. 0171 613 5580

frank love

The Dairy
5-7 Marischal Road
London
SE13 5LE

t. 0181 297 2212
f. 0181 297 2212

241
GB

title
Lust pants
medium
Mixed media
purpose of work
Self promotional

agent
Eastwing
98 Columbia Road
London
E2 7QB
t. 0171 613 5580

327
.

jan lewis

1 Coombe End
Whitchurch Hill
Pangbourne
Berks
RG8 7TE

t. 01189 842590
f. 01189 842590

242
GB

title
The Princess and
the Halibut
medium
Watercolour / ink
purpose of work
Children's story
(unfinished)

brief
A variation on a
theme! This
illustration is taken
from a story for
children which tells
the tale from the
point of view of an
enchanted halibut!

itle
A Day Out

medium
Acrylic on board

purpose of work
Self promotional

brief
To produce a figure
study, working on
a larger scale than
normal and
utilising more
texture

agent
The Inkshed
98 Columbia Road
London
E2 7QB
t. 0171 613 2323

brigitte mcdonald

40 Knightlow Road
Harborne
Birmingham
B17 8QB

t. 0121 429 8655
f. 0121 429 8655

title
Love Bird
medium
Water colour and
gouache
purpose of work
Speculative
greetings card / self
promotional

brief
To illustrate a
range of cards
using a Love theme

shane mcgowan

23A Parkholme
Road
London
E8 3AG

t. 0171 249 6444
f. 0171 249 6444

title
Fatboy rides again
medium
Gouache, ink
purpose of work
Self promotional
Christmas card
brief
Do something jazzy
agent
The Organisation
69 Caledonian
Road
London N1
t. 0171 833 8268

belle mellor

Flat 3,
12 Lansdowne Street
Hove
East Sussex
BN3 1FQ

t. 01273 732604
f. 01273 732604
mobile. 0973 463942

246

GB

title
Horse Woman
medium
Pen and Ink, gold
powder, rubber
stamps
purpose of work
Self promotion

brief
Produce a card to
inform clients of
my return from
India

rosalyn mina

20 The Castle
Horsham
West Sussex
RH12 5PX

t. 01403 217230

title
Autumn

medium
Mono - print and pastel

purpose of work
Self Promotional

brief
'Autumn' is part of a self promotional series illustrating the four seasons. My main aim was to create rich textures and vibrant colours

george parfitt

51 Melody Road
London
SW18 2QW

t. 0181 874 5314

248

GB

title
Noel and Liam

medium
Pen, ink, gouache

purpose of work
Self promotional

brief
A caricature portrait
of Liam and Noel
Gallagher, of the
group 'Oasis'

sophia please

185 Peperharow
Road
Godalming
Surrey
GU7 2PR

t. 01483 421596

249
GB

title
Let a Thousand
Flowers Bloom

medium
Photography

purpose of work
Article for
New Scientist

brief
To produce a
colour image for an
article on how
flowers can
detoxify
contaminated
industrial sites

ian pollock

171 Bond Street
Macclesfield
Cheshire
SK11 6RE

t. 01625 426205
f. 01625 261390

250

GB

The Sower   Ian Pollock

title
The Sower
medium
Watercolour ink
and gouache

brief
One of 40
illustrations for
"The Parables of
Christ"
agent
The Inkshed
98 Columbia Road
London
E2 7QB
t. 0171 613 2323

paul powis

Four Seasons
74 Battenhall
Avenue
Worcester
WR5 2HW

t. 01905 357563
f. 01905 357563

251

GB

UNPUBLISHED

title
River

medium
Acrylic

purpose of work
Self Promotional

brief
To capture summer
landscape and river

matthew richardson

Garden Cottage
Penpont
Brecon, Powys
LD3 8EU

t. 01874 636269
f. 01874 636269

252
GB

title
School Ties

medium
Mixed

purpose of work
Editorial illustration

brief
Illustrating a piece
about a college
reunion which turns
into a lecture and
demand for college
funding

matthew richardson

Garden Cottage
Penpont
Brecon, Powys
LD3 8EU

t. 01874 636269
f. 01874 636269

title
Fly - Boy

medium
Mixed

purpose of work
Self promotional

brief
Experimental and
developmental

johanne ryder

The Dairy
5-7 Marischal Road
London
SE13 5LE

t. 0181 297 2212
f. 0181 297 2212

254
GB

title
Financial Growth
medium
Clay, paper,
Photoshop 4
purpose of work
Self promotional
brief
Developing
personal work

peter till

11 Berkeley Road
London
N8 8RU

t. 0181 341 0497
f. 0181 341 0497

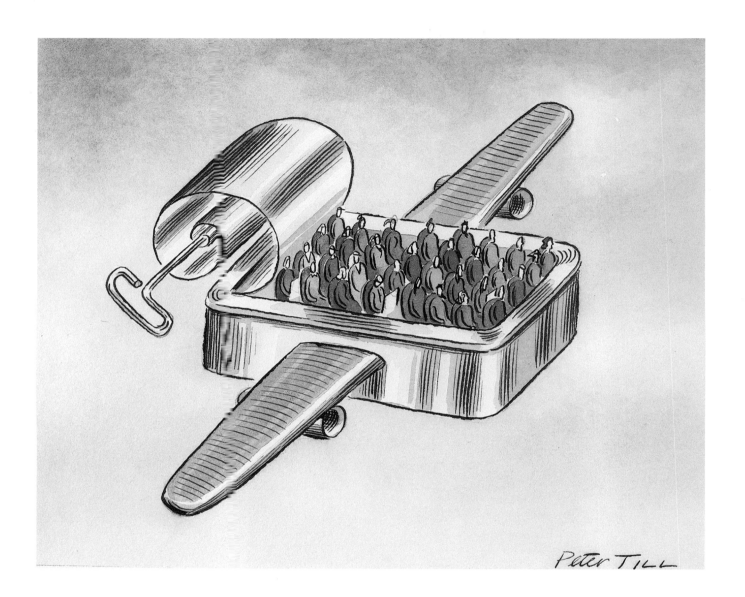

title
Sardine Airlines
medium
Pen, ink and
watercolour
purpose of work
To illustrate article

brief
Piece about
overcrowded
planes
commissioned by
Deborah De Staffan
company
Town and Country

helen wakefield

36 Courtenay Ave
Belmont Heights
Sutton
Surrey
SM2 5ND

t. 0181 643 0040
f. 0181 770 1884

title
Mad for it

medium
Mixed Media

purpose of work
Self promotional

brief
Portrait of Liam
Gallagher

alan young

2 Chapel Cottages
Dunks Green
Tonbridge
Kent
TN11 9SF

t. 01732 810652
f. 01622 621100

257

GB

title
Shadow of the
Forest
medium
Watercolour
purpose of work
Self promotional
brief
To respond to the
idea of culture and
wilderness in
Finland